Tokaj

A COMPANION
FOR THE BIBULOUS TRAVELLER

By David Copp
Introduction by Hugh Johnson OBE

Tokaj

A COMPANION FOR THE BIBULOUS TRAVELLER

By David Copp

Introduction by Hugh Johnson OBE

PXB

Budapest, 2007

Tokaj: A Companion for the Bibulous Traveller
by David Copp

Editor: Nick Robertson

Picture editor: Bianca Otero

Design: Anna Lőrincz, Zsolt Zimmermann

Layout: Réka Fülöp

Pictures: Bianca Otero, Fekete K.

Maps: Ede András Molnár

Editorial contributor: Robert Smyth

Production: Péter Wunderlich

Published by: PrintXBudavár Zrt., H-1061 Budapest, Király u. 16,
Hungary. Tel.: +36 (1) 887 4848

ISBN 978 963 87524 3 7

Printed by: Prospektus Nyomda, Veszprém

Printed in Hungary, 2007

Contents

Foreword

THE YEARS SINCE 1989 have seen the gradual revelation of the Hungary that was legend before the World Wars and communism of the last century. Budapest is revealed again as one of Europe's grandest and most stylish capitals, its people, its arts, its atmosphere and its provisions original, marvellous and vaut le voyage.

EVEN BEFORE BUDAPEST got back on its feet, though, there were stirrings in the remote northeast of the country where a wine long recognised as one of the world's most desirable had been languishing unloved. Tokaj is as much a feast of Hungary's national image as Budapest, Bartók, paprika and tempestuous violins.

IT WAS THE FIRST, and for centuries among the most expensive, of the world's great sweet wines, credited with miraculous qualities – aphrodisiac, lifesaver, and the ultimate gift from monarch to monarch. The comparison with Burgundy is inevitable: a rural region and its villages promoted to the world stage by the produce of its fields.

TOKAJ'S YELLOW-PAINTED buildings in country-Baroque could be almost anywhere in Central Europe; its forests and rivers are the essence of the heart of the continent. Yet nowhere else shares its singular climate, the sun and mist of its autumns, the grapes that profit by them, and the miles of rock-cut tunnels that form its labyrinthine cellars. Those elements, the Tokaj people, their unique culture, their monuments and their hospitality are the subject of this book.

THE REAWAKENING of Tokaj has been an extraordinary phenomenon. Capital has poured in (from France above all), new transport links have brought it to within easy reach of Budapest, fine hotels and restaurants have opened, and in 2002 the whole region was declared a World Heritage Site.

I ARRIVED IN TOKAJ IN 1989. It was cold, hungry and depressed. Eighteen years later it has a spring in its step, and everything to offer the visitor. David Copp knows the region and its wines well, and his Companion will make your visit doubly rewarding.

Hugh Johnson OBE

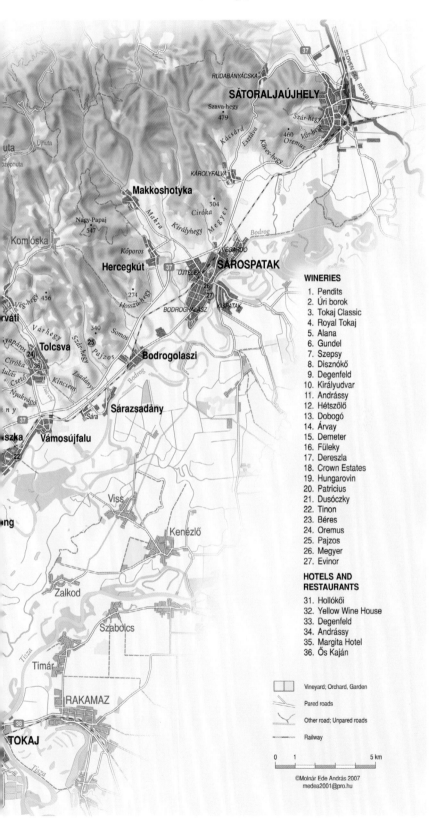

WINERIES

1. Pendits
2. Úri borok
3. Tokaj Classic
4. Royal Tokaj
5. Alana
6. Gundel
7. Szepsy
8. Disznókő
9. Degenfeld
10. Királyudvar
11. Andrássy
12. Hétszőlő
13. Dobogó
14. Árvay
15. Demeter
16. Füleky
17. Dereszla
18. Crown Estates
19. Hungarovin
20. Patricius
21. Dusóczky
22. Tinon
23. Béres
24. Oremus
25. Pajzos
26. Megyer
27. Evinor

HOTELS AND RESTAURANTS

31. Hollókői
32. Yellow Wine House
33. Degenfeld
34. Andrássy
35. Margita Hotel
36. Ős Kaján

Vineyard; Orchard, Garden

Pared roads

Other road; Unpared roads

Railway

0 1   5 km

©Molnár Ede András 2007
medea2001@pro.hu

Introduction

THE TIMELESS LITTLE TOWN of Tokaj has a thoroughly unpretentious air. Its narrow, cobbled streets and faded yellow Baroque buildings make it appear modest, and yet it is the capital of one of the world's most revered wine-making regions.

TOKAJ MAY NOT COMPARE in size with Bordeaux, Beaune, Oporto or Jerez, but like those cities it possesses a long and rich history, and like them has made a significant contribution to European wine culture. Its venerable status was universally acknowledged when the region was declared a UNESCO World Heritage Site, honouring its distinctive landscape and thousand-year-long viticultural tradition.

GREAT WINE EVOLVES FROM LANDSCAPE. In Tokaj the combination of volcanic soils, extraordinary climatic conditions, long-established cultivars and deep, cool cellars all contribute to an ideal winemaking environment providing great Aszú wines. Such a landscape has inspired generations of vintners.

THIS COMPANION sets out to explore the landscape, history and culture that made Tokaj world-famous, taking you into its most revered vineyards and introducing you to the winemakers that have done so much to restore the quality and reputation of its wines.

TOKAJ is not only the name of the town but also of the region known in Hungarian as Tokaj-Hegyalja – the Tokaji Foothills. The gentle slopes of the Zemplén Range are the lower hills of the mighty Carpathians, the mountains protecting the fertile Carpathian Basin from cold northern winds and nourishing its soils with fresh, fast-running water.

THE WINE that made the region famous is Tokaji Aszú (pronounced 'ossu'), one of the world's most remarkable libations. 'Aszú' is best translated as 'shrivelled grapes'. In autumn before the harvest, Tokaj's unique microclimate causes a 'noble rot' to attack the grapes, making them shrivel – but instead of being harmed, the fruit is endowed with benefits that contribute to making wonderfully elegant and delicate wines.

WE BEGIN by exploring the unique conditions that nature has assembled in Tokaj, the history of the land and its people, and the range of wines produced, and then suggest how to get the best from this Companion.

OUR PRINCIPAL purpose is to enhance your enjoyment of a visit to the Tokaji area and its wineries. It is quite a compact region with most of the wineries and great vineyards within a radius of 25 kilometres from Tokaj town.

THE BOOK is designed to help those who wish to make their own itineraries and we hope that it will also be a trusted companion to those on organised tours who want additional background information about Tokaji wines and wineries.

WE HAVE DIVIDED the region into four areas – Tokaj Hill, the Mád Basin, Erdő-bénye and Tolcsva, and Sárospatak. We start from Tokaj Hill and give directions to the other areas with Tokaj town as a starting point.

ALONG WITH SOME BASIC TRAVEL information we summarise the history of
late-harvest wines, describe the soil, climate and grape varieties planted,
and explain the range of wines produced and how they might be enjoyed.

THE MAIN BODY OF THE BOOK is given to a description of the wineries,
how to find them and what facilities they offer visitors. In each of the
four areas we list the largest wineries first because they generally are best
geared to receive visitors (although please note that some of them host
trade visits only by appointment). We also list many of the up-and-com-
ing small family wineries where you will be warmly welcomed and find
some very exciting wines.

THE MAPS for each area show the main wineries, hotels, restaurants and
leisure facilities, as well as the greatest of the classified vineyards.

The Land

LANDSCAPE

THE TOKAJI REGION WAS FORMED about 15 million years ago when a tectonic fault caused 1,000 or more volcanoes to erupt, depositing lava that was to provide a base of hard igneous rock.

SEVERAL MILLION years later the region was submerged by the Mare Magnum (Great Sea) that has since receded to form the Mediterranean, leaving behind valuable clay and marine deposits. Later volcanic action then brought wind-borne deposits of loess.

THE THREE MOST BASIC soil types you will find in Tokaj are clay, clay mixed with broken rock (locally known as *nyirok*), and loess, a windblown loamy soil. Occasionally you will come across other soils such as the fine-grained rock flour formed by silicified rock and pumice.

CLAY SOILS yield full-bodied wines such as those from Király in Mád. Nyirok soils, such as those in Lapis near Bodrogkeresztúr, give wines with very fine acids and a distinctive character. Loess, sometimes referred to as yellow earth, is mainly found around Tokaj Hill and produces refined and elegant wines with an attractive honeyed aroma.

CLIMATE

LOCATED AT GLOBAL coordinates 48N 21E, Tokaj has clearly defined seasons. Winters are short and sharp and followed by early springs and warm summers. However, it is the region's long sunny autumns, allowing the grapes to ripen well into October and November, that make Tokaji wines so special.

IN THE AUTUMN, the summer heat generated by the Great Hungarian Plain hovers over the cool waters of the Bodrog and Tisza rivers, their water meadows and marshes causing heavy morning mists.

WHEN THESE MISTS are dispersed by warm midmorning sunshine, the combination of humidity and warm air causes the thin skin of the grapes to

split, allowing the moisture in them to gradually seep away, which leaves the grapes full of concentrated sugar and fine organic acids.

THE MIRACLE OF TOKAJ happens when a 'noble rot' (*botrytis cinerea* in Latin) forms on the ripe grapes, sealing them and expelling potentially harmful microorganisms.

WHEN THE 'ROTTEN' berries are carefully handpicked and gently pressed under their own weight, the resultant grape juice contains four or five times the normal sugar content. This high natural sweetness is balanced with extremely fine natural acids produced by the grapes being grown in volcanic soils. It is the balance of sugar and acid in Aszú wines that make them so exceptional to taste. The natural sugar is not cloying but wonderfully refined, making exquisite and elegant wines.

TERROIR

TERROIR IS A FRENCH WORD that has no precise English translation. It is generally accepted to define a holistic combination of several components of a viticultural site, such as soil, climate, sunlight energy, hydrology and topography (i.e. altitude), aspect, and angle of slope. French and Tokaji vignerons believe that terroir is the most important factor in making fine wines that develop in the bottle over a long period of time. It is not surprising that five of the largest Tokaji wineries are French-owned.

THE TOKAJI GROWERS were the first to classify their vineyards. The original classification was based on the quality of botrytised fruit produced. Sweetness was considered something special in an age when sugar was a costly luxury.

TODAY, classification values are usually based on other factors such as heat summation and the character of wine produced. Classification authorities consider a wine's complexity, depth and character. We believe that most of the originally classified Tokaji vineyards would still qualify on these criteria because their mineral-rich, volcanic soils warm up quickly, enjoy a long growing season, and produce wines of great individual character.

THE BEST VINEYARDS in the northern hemisphere tend to be found midway up well-drained south-facing slopes between 120 and 240 metres above sea level. They are quite easy to identify because they are usually just below the tree line and protected by wooded hills from cold northerly winds.

THESE SITES have always been sought-after and vintners recognised their special character by making single-vineyard wines. However, after 1713 (when Hungary's Rákóczi-led revolution was quelled) different landowners with less-reverent perspectives took over. They were more interested in developing estates than protecting the integrity of a particular terroir. Following the earlier example of the Garay Family at Hétszőlő, they merged several vineyards into one and gave the whole the name of the most famous site within the conglomerated land.

THE ROYAL TOKAJ WINERY deserves credit for reintroducing the single-vineyard concept in the post-communist period, producing dedicated wines from each of three First Growth vineyards and one Great Growth, Mézes Mály. Since then many other vintners have produced single-vineyard wines from exceptional growths, such as Királyudvar from their Lapis Vineyard that was nominated Champion Wine at the 2007 Pannon Bormustra (Pannon Wine Festival), the most prestigious Hungarian fine-wine competition.

WE BELIEVE that there is a case for the reclassification of the best terroirs, even though it would mean redefining the area of some that were expanded beyond their original size. As things stand, the two Great Growths – Mézes Mály and Szarvas – are the Tokaji equivalent of Burgundy's Le Montrachet and Romanee-Conti vineyards. It's possible that three or four other vineyards could be considered of equal status. Whatever the future of Tokaji classification we sincerely hope that you will be able to visit some of the best vineyards, taste their wines, and enjoy forming your own opinion on the matter.

The People

A REFINED HISTORY
OF TOKAJ AND ITS WINES

Origins of Late-Harvest Wines

IN ANTIQUITY LATE-HARVEST WINES were admired for their flavour and nutritional content. The grapes were picked as late as possible and sun-dried on mats until they shrivelled. The resultant wines, intensely sweet and powerful, were considered to be the nectar of the gods.

STORED IN AMPHORAE in the ground and opened for the Spring Festival of the wine god Dionysus, the wines were usually consumed before warmer weather caused a secondary fermentation that reduced their natural sugar content.

THE BEST RAISIN WINES were produced in the volcanic soils of Crete and Santorini, and in the Peloponnesus. The Venetians, the pre-eminent Mediterranean trading power of the Middle Ages, considered them the most valuable of all wines and called them Malvasia.

THE PRACTICE of making sweet wines spread through the Balkans into Szerémség in southern Hungary (part of today's Serbia), where the wines became famous. Indeed, by 1450 the Moldovan ruler invited Janos

Cotnari to bring Hungarian cultivars to establish late-harvest winemaking in his country.

ABOUT THE SAME TIME, the little village of Rust on the western lakefront of the Neusiedler See in Hungary became so famous for its late-harvest wines that King Matthias (1458-1490) granted it a market and later conferred upon Rust the status of a chartered town.

Tokaji Rises to Prominence

TOKAJ DEVELOPED RAPIDLY after 1500 because many southern Hungarian landowners with wine interests moved north out of the path of the Ottoman armies advancing on Vienna. Tokaji was the ideal location for making sweet wines because of the excellent conditions for botrytis and also because it was at the crossroads of multidirectional trade routes.

AT THAT TIME sugar was an expensive luxury in Europe. Wines with a high residual sugar content were in great demand by those with the money to buy them. The problem for winemakers, however, was stabilising wines containing such high levels of residual sugar before they started a secondary fermentation in warmer weather, thereby reducing the natural sugar content.

THE BREAKTHROUGH came sometime around the middle of the 16th century, when Tokaji growers realised that the noble rot concentrated the sugar in some grapes but did not affect them all. Experimentation revealed that if the rotten grapes were collected and vinified separately from the others, the resulting wine would have four or five times as much residual sugar – enough to halt secondary fermentation.

HOWEVER, such a concentrated and expensive wine would limit its market, so vintners macerated the botrytised grapes in a wine made from the non-botrytised grapes. By further experimentation they found that above 60g/l sugar, the wine remained stable and that the sugar acted as a preservative.

IT IS NOW BELIEVED that the term 'Aszú' became current in the latter half of the 16th century. The historian István Zelenák unearthed a Garay Family document dated 1571 that states decisively: "I lay no claim of any kind to the 70 barrels and 52 casks of Aszú wine in the Tokaji cellar of my dear brother." The renowned scholar Balázs Fabricius also used the term in a book published in 1576. However, it is generally accepted that the first person to write down a detailed method of making Aszú wines was amateur vintner Laczkó Szepsi, chaplain to the Rákóczi Family.

The Rákóczi Legacy

THE RÁKÓCZI NAME first became synonymous with Tokaj when Zsigmond Rákóczi (1544-1608) was granted land around Szerencs for his part in the wars against the Turks, and later became Regent and then Prince of Transylvania.

HIS SON GYÖRGY I (1593-1648) married into the wealthy Lórántffy Family and acquired Sárospatak Castle, which he extended and made the family home. In 1630, he followed the celebrated Gábor Bethlen as ruling Prince of Transylvania and made Sárospatak the centre of the political, economic and cultural life of the region. Rákóczi strengthened the ties between Northern or Royal Hungary and Transylvania.

ALSO IN 1630, Chaplain Szepsi gave an Aszú wine that he had made to Zsuzsanna Lórántffy, wife of György I. Rákóczi was quick to realise the commercial and diplomatic potential for Aszú wines, and became adept at persuading the great and the grand of Europe to endorse them. Tokaj wine

became fashionable at the courts of the kings and queens of Poland, Russia, Sweden and France, its popularity boosted by claims that the wines had both medicinal and aphrodisiacal properties.

AS THE RÁKÓCZI FAMILY PROSPERED, György II (1648-57) and Ferenc I (1657-76) also became Princes of Transylvania – but it is Ferenc Rákóczi II (1676-1735) that Hungarians recall most vividly, and consider a national hero.

FERENC II WAS BORN the son of Ferenc I and Ilona Zrínyi who, on the premature death of her husband, married the great freedom-fighter Imre Thököly. At first his brave mother took charge of her son's education in the family's various castles in northeastern Hungary. However, because of his parents' declaration for Hungarian independence from the Habsburgs, the Emperor put Ferenc II under the charge of Jesuits in Vienna.

AFTER HIS MARRIAGE, he was allowed to return to northeastern Hungary to take over his inheritance – vast estates, including many of the finest Tokaji vineyards. He worked hard, expanding and modernising them, and in 1700 agreed with other important landowners to a classification of the Tokaji vineyards – believed to be the first-ever recorded terroir classification in the world. This classification was the basis of all subsequent classifications, including the one now embodied in Hungarian wine law.

FERENC II ALSO INVESTED in businesses such as glass foundries and sawmills. In those days the demand for glass windows for draughty castles was greater than that for wine bottles. Glass bottles were extremely expensive and only used for bottling valuable Tokaji essencia wines that were given as princely gifts. There was also a large demand for wooden barrels made from the sessile oak of the Zemplén forests, because wine was generally sold and transported in small 136-litre barrels.

THE EXPULSION of the last Turks from Hungary in 1699 increased Hungarian desire for independence from the Habsburgs. Encouraged by the French, who were seeking allies against the Austrians in their bid for greater balance of power in Europe, the independent-minded aristocracy and peasantry alike turned to Ferenc II for leadership.

WHEN THE WAR of the Spanish Succession (1701-1714) broke out between

the French and the Habsburgs, the French King Louis XIV agreed to support the Hungarian fight for freedom in return for the Hungarians harrying the Habsburgs from the east.

FERENC II DECLARED the Hungarian War of Independence in 1703, but the unexpected defeat of the French at Blenheim the following year meant the end of French support.

RÁKÓCZI'S BRAVE ARMY fought on for another seven years before its surrender. All Rákóczi land, including the prized vineyards, was appropriated by the Austrian Treasury, and Rákóczi spent the remainder of his life in exile.

FERENC II IS REVERED because he was a sincere and honourable man. Like his mother and stepfather he was a courageous leader who embodied the spirit of freedom. It is largely because of him that the family name graces the streets, squares and buildings of almost every Hungarian town and village – along with many Tokaji wines and destinations.

ONLY ONE of the Rákóczi Family's legacies was that the 17th and 18th centuries were a golden age for Tokaji wine producers, who led the world in three different aspects of winemaking and trading.

TOKAJI VINTNERS were the first to classify their vineyards by terroir. It is true that the classification was made according to the capacity of a site to consistently produce well-botrytised grapes. However, the first classification, made in 1700, was apparently so precise that it has served as the basis of all subsequent classifications, including the official classification of 1772 that was embodied into Hungarian wine law.

SECONDLY, Tokaji landlords recognised the importance of skilled workers in the vineyard. While most of Europe toiled under serfdom, the enlightened Tokaji landlords understood that cultivating and harvesting botrytised grapes was a labour-intensive task better encouraged than enforced. They introduced a system by which skilled workers were compensated for completing a set of viticultural tasks in a specific area of the vineyard that resulted in a higher quality of botrytised grapes. As a result, the best and most adept vineyard workers were attracted to Tokaji.

THIRDLY, due to the skills required to grow, vinify and mature complex Aszú wines successfully, Tokaj produced a stream of world-class oenologists who continually developed and finessed their winemaking techniques.

Hard Times to Modern Times

THE NAPOLEONIC WARS, the division of Poland, and the rise of Prussia brought an end to the golden age. Increasing competition from other sweet wines made trade more difficult. The Dutch Cape Colony at Constantia became famous for its sweet wines, as did the Rhine and Moselle valleys and Chateau d'Yquem in the Sauternes district of southwest France.

MATTERS WENT from bad to worse for Tokaji producers in the 19th and 20th centuries. The 1848-49 War of Independence ended in disaster for the Hungarians, and in 1885 the root-louse phylloxera devastated the best Tokaji vineyards. It took 20 years to find and develop disease-free rootstock and replant the vineyards, and the hard work had just about been completed when the First World War broke out. At the end of it Hungary lost two-thirds of its territory, including all of Transylvania, the most important domestic market for Tokaji wines.

DURING THE SECOND WORLD WAR, Nazis drove Jewish wine traders out of Tokaj, and immediately afterwards Hungary became subject to the communist sphere of influence. The great private estates were nationalised and amalgamated into the state-owned Borkombinát. Many of the most experienced landowners, vintners and traders left Tokaj, and the traditional methods of winemaking were replaced by those of a command economy.

THUS FOR 50 YEARS AFTER 1939, Tokaji Aszú became the forgotten wine of Europe. However, in 1990 the first modern democratic Hungarian government was elected and moved decisively to decentralise and privatise the wine industry and attract foreign and Hungarian investment.

IT IS ESTIMATED THAT SINCE 1990 some 250 million euros have been invested in Tokaj for the purchase and replanting of vineyards, and the building of brand-new state-of-the-art wineries. Seventeen years later, after a great deal of hard work, Tokaj is poised to reenter world markets with a superb range of wines made with the advantages of modern technology, yet retaining the traditional standards of the pre-communist period. Now is the optimal time to visit Tokaj to see its bountiful vineyards, taste its fine wines, and meet its best winemakers.

TOKAJ RENAISSANCE

IN 1995 EIGHT of the leading wineries owning classified vineyards formed the Tokaj Renaissance Association to restore the reputation of Aszú wines. The original members have since been joined by ten others equally determined to uphold the highest standards of viticulture and viniculture, and there are at least another 30 small family wineries equally committed to the same cause. Most of these wineries own plots in the renowned classified vineyards that produce wines of generous character and great longevity.

THIS COMPANION emphasises the importance of terroir in making great – as opposed to simply good – wines. The best vineyards are shown on our maps, and basic information is provided about them on the pages devoted to the leading wineries with which they are most closely associated. We believe that you will find walking in the vineyards will enhance your knowledge and understanding of Tokaji wines.

THE TOKAJ RENAISSANCE Association actively promotes Tokaji wines in several key Western markets. Look out for opportunities to taste associates' wines in your own country; log on to www.tokaji.hu to learn more. The Association has new offices in Tokaj at Dózsa György utca 5 (T: +36 47 353 612).

WOMEN WINEMAKERS OF TOKAJ

TOKAJ HAS A HIGHER PROPORTION OF WOMEN engaged in winemaking than other Hungarian wine regions, and a number of their libations are rated very highly indeed by the male winemaking fraternity.

THERE IS A THEORY that women are more naturally talented at dealing with the intricacies of such a complex wine as Tokaji Aszú, but it can be equally argued that a number of male vintners are in touch with their feminine side. Nevertheless, women such as Márta Wille-Baumkauff, Stéphanie Berecz, Sarolta Bárdos, and Judit Bott are making elegant, delicate, sophisticated Aszú wines that have something very feminine about them.

BERECZ, who hails from France and trained at leading Tokaji estate Disznókő, now has her own company which she runs with her husband Zsolt. Research has shown that women of childbearing age generally

have a more precise tasting capacity than men, and Berecz believes that there are several stages in the Tokaj winemaking process where this capacity can be used to make decisions that can positively affect development of the wines and lead to greater vinicultural creativity.

KATALIN HUDACSKÓ, Zsuzsanna Bene, and Ildikó Posta have a similar touch in making wines for their family firms. Their wines may look heavy and oxidized in the glass, but they are very soft and graceful in the mouth.

THE TOKAJI BORBORÁTNŐK (loosely translated as 'Girlfriends of Tokaji Wine') was formed in Mád in December 2003 and includes female winemakers; wives, sisters and daughters of famous vintners; wine marketers; educators; and food and wine correspondents. Their main aim is to spread the good name of Tokaji, and to increase the effectiveness of their mission they have become affiliated with the International Women in Wine Association.

THE 'GIRLFRIENDS' have been particularly successful at promoting wine drinking in connection with gastronomy, work in which Gabriella Mészáros (the leading Hungarian-wine educator) and Helga Gál (a consultant at TV Paprika) are very actively involved.

APPROPRIATELY, the annual charity ball of the Tokaji Borborátnők is a tour de force of matching food and wine. Being an equal-opportunity organization, the 'Girlfriends' invited a team of male chefs to prepare the 2006 banquet that preceded the ball, and selected wines made by male vintners.

ALL AGREED that the pairing of István Szepsy's mineral-rich, single-vineyard 2005 Szent Tamás Dry Furmint with scallops and asparagus ragout, served with creamy beetroot sauce and leek, was inspired. The evening was a great success.

THE 'GIRLFRIENDS' have already made a valuable contribution to the world renaissance of Tokaji wines with their genuine enthusiasm for the cause.

The Wine

VITICULTURE

TENDING A VINEYARD is a year-round task which commences immediately after the vintage, when the soil is fertilised (preferably with organic compound) to sustain the concentration of active acidity and revitalise microbial life.

ONCE THE HARVEST IS gathered the vineyards are ploughed to allow winter rains to permeate the soil. The base of the vine is covered with earth as protection against winter frosts.

WINTER PRUNING begins once the vine becomes dormant. The general rule is that the more severe the pruning, the better the grown fruit's quality.

PRUNING CONTINUES into February and March, when cuttings are taken from healthy plants for grafting onto new, disease-free rootstock to be planted out the following year.

IN MARCH the vines begin to wake from winter hibernation and sap starts to rise. The soil is aerated by ploughing, and maintenance work on vine posts and training wires is undertaken. When the soil begins to warm up the one-year-old vines are planted out.

THREE TO FOUR WEEKS after the sap has started to rise the buds form. They come to flower seven or eight weeks later at the end of May or beginning of June, depending on weather conditions. Flowering is the most important period in the viticultural calendar and ideally it takes place in a warm, dry, and above all frost-free period.

IN JUNE the soil is loosened again to aerate roots and discourage dormant pests. Spraying with copper sulphate reduces the threat of the most common vine diseases, such as mildew.

WHEN THE FLOWERING is complete the best shoots are selected and trained along trellis wires. The most widely used training system is the low single-cordon that allows bunches to retain the warmth of the earth and be exposed to sunlight.

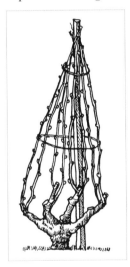

THE MAIN TASK IN JULY AND AUGUST is to encourage the growth of healthy bunches by cutting back excessive vegetation, and trimming away wild

shoots and unhealthy or damaged fruit so that selected bunches get the best possible exposure to sunshine and warmth.

IN SEPTEMBER harvesting equipment is prepared. The first grapes to be picked are those for making dry white wines because acidity is vital to their freshness and fruitiness. The longer grapes stay on

the vine the better their aroma and flavour will develop in the barrel. However, the grower has to decide the optimum time for picking each vineyard, when the grapes have the right sugar/acid balance for the style of wine to be made.

WINEMAKING

MOST DRY AND SEMISWEET wines are now made by the reductive method, which reduces the exposure of the grape juice (must) to oxygen and enhances the primary fruit flavours of the wine. After controlled and gentle pressing the must is immediately fed into temperature-controlled stainless steel fermentation tanks, where the yeasts on the skins begin to react with the natural sugars in the grape.

WINES THAT ARE TO BE barrel-fermented are poured into new or used oak.

Barrel-fermented wines that are allowed to rest on their lees for several weeks generally have more body than those fermented in steel tanks.

THE PROCESS FOR LATE-HARVEST WINES is quite different. The grapes for late-harvest and Szamorodni wines are picked by the bunch (including some botrytised grapes and some that are not – hence the term 'as they come') and brought to the winery, de-stalked, and fed into a vat where they are left on their skins until they get the desired colour, and then gently pressed.

FERMENTATION converts the natural sugar into alcohol over a period of 10-20 days. When the fermentation has been completed the wines are racked off their lees before being returned to stainless steel tanks, or barrels if the wine is to be barrel-matured.

WHEN MAKING THE GREAT ASZÚ WINES the vintner will only use handpicked botrytised berries that have the ideal sugar/acid balance. The best berries are generally chocolate-brown in colour with yellow-brown pulp and seeds. They are brought to the winery as quickly as possible and piled into vats (wooden or stainless steel) where they are pressed by their own weight. The first-run juice, called Essencia, usually starts to flow after 24-36 hours and is often drawn off and fermented separately.

THE ASZÚ BERRIES in the vat are then gently pressed (to avoid damaging the pips) and macerated with a base wine made from ripe but non-botrytised grapes. The wine is then matured in wood for a minimum of two years. The high residual sugar content of the grape juice and the low cellar temperatures means that fermentation is slow.

DURING FERMENTATION the volume of wine decreases. Tokaji vintners found that if the barrels were not topped-up, the rich store of natural yeasts and bacteria would feed on the wine and weave a web of flavours that gave the wine added complexity and character. This gentle and controlled oxidation of Aszú wines was the method used for centuries by Tokaji vintners who understood the important part that the cellar environment played in the process. The soft volcanic rock, constant low temperature, and high humidity combined to generate unique microflora.

SADLY, bad practices crept in during the communist period, such as over-oxidation, pasteurisation, and the addition of alcohol to mask deficiencies in the wine. Although these methods have been eliminated, there is a tendency to associate the malpractices of the communist period with the centuries-old traditional methods of making Aszú.

MANY MODERN VINTNERS believe that their prime task in making Aszú wines is to encourage natural fruit aromas and flavours by reducing the amount of oxidation. They also feel that the reductive process allows better expression of the natural character of the terroir.

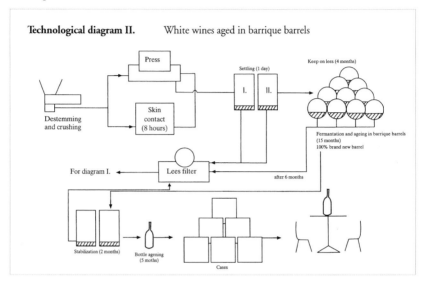

THUS THERE ARE AT LEAST TWO DISTINCT ASZÚ STYLES, modern and traditional, the latter being slightly more oxidative. We recommend that while you are in Tokaji, try both styles and keep an open mind.

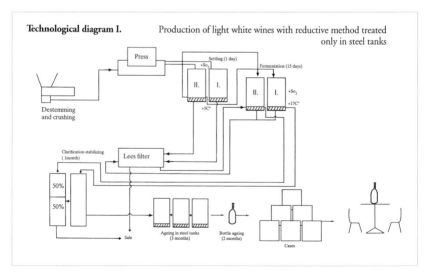

WE CONSIDER that it would be a great disadvantage for Tokaji producers to be shackled to a one-dimensional view of how Aszú wine should be made. We also feel that it is in the consumer interest that winemakers remain free to express their own stylistic ideas within the framework of the wine law.

VINEYARD NAMES

ETYMOLOGICAL NAMES for vineyards have developed from people, animals, places, trees, geographical features, religion, and even a racehorse.

HONOURING SOME OF HUNGARY'S HISTORICAL NOTABLES, vineyards named after Rákóczi, Szepsy, Teleki, Terézia, and Deák grace the landscape. Szarvas ('deer'), Disznókő ('wild boar'), and Nyulászó ('running hares') indicates the prevalent wildlife. Local produce like Szilvás ('plums'), Cseresznye ('cherries'), and Mandulás ('almonds') abound – and vineyardists consider almond trees a sign of a good, warm site.

HÉTSZŐLŐ ('SEVEN VINEYARDS') AND VÁRHEGY ('CASTLE HILL') are self-evidently named, while religious considerations were almost certainly inspirational for Oremus, Szent Tamás, Remete ('hermit'), Szentvér ('holy blood'), and Szentkereszt ('holy cross').

MÉZES MÁLY ('HONEY POT') refers to the honeyed aromas and flavours of wines from that vineyard, while Zafír ('sapphire') was named after a Jewish wine merchant and jeweller. And Kincsem ('my treasure') pays tribute to Hungary's greatest racehorse.

GRAPE VARIETIES

THE CULTIVARS that thrive best in Tokaji soils and provide the best botrytised grapes are Furmint, Hárslevelű, Muscat, Zéta and Kövérszőlő. Kabar, a cross of Bouvier with Hárslevelű, was authorised for making Tokaji appellation wines beginning in January 2007.

FURMINT is by far the most important of these six varieties. No one knows its specific origin, yet it has come to dominate Tokaji plantings because winemakers appreciate its perfect match to the soil and climatic conditions, and because it can be relied on to give structure and backbone to their wines. When the grapes are fully ripe they impart a lovely rich flavour to the wines and provide fine, natural acids that keep the wine fresh over a very long period.

FURMINT GROWS VIGOROUSLY, ripens late, and thrives in volcanic soils. Its thin skin splits readily when humidity is combined

with late autumn sunshine, developing botrytis cinerea. It is recognizable by its long cylindrical bunches that hang gracefully from the trained shoots of the vine.

HÁRSLEVELŰ is an ancient Hungarian variety that is an indispensable marriage partner to Furmint, as its linden-flower and honey aromas and more elegant acids add warmth and fragrance to blends.

HÁRSLEVELŰ LIKES VOLCANIC SOILS but also thrives in loess, producing rich, full-bodied wines. It has different water requirements than Furmint and is normally planted around the skirt of a hill where there is greater moisture in the ground.

ITS NAME DERIVES from its linden leaf, and the vines provide large clusters of smaller berries in looser bunches than the Furmint.

SÁRGA MUSKOTÁLY OR YELLOW MUSCAT is probably the oldest variety in the Carpathian Basin, and was widely used at the time of the Roman occupation of Pannonia. It has vigourous acids, but its real contribution is the richness of its aroma and body, and its generous mouth-filling taste.

IT IS A MIDSEASON, medium-to-heavy fruit-bearing variety that is quite demanding in terms of soil and climate (it needs protection from frost), and requires harvesting at a relatively low sugar-must level of 17-18 grams per litre.

IT CAN BE RECOGNISED by the yellowness of its skin and its compact clusters. This variety is also referred to as Muscat Lunel or Muscat Blanc a Petits Grains.

ZÉTA, formerly known as Oremus, is a cross of Furmint with Bouvier that ripens early and botrytises well. It does not have quite the same steely, mineral backbone of the Furmint but it is useful insurance against poor late-autumn weather. It blends happily with its more celebrated cousin and can be recognised by its neat conical clusters. It is rarely marketed as a standalone wine because its acidity declines rapidly.

KÖVÉRSZŐLŐ, also known as Graso de Cotnari, is called the 'fat grape' because of its good size and its rich, generous flavours. The variety almost disappeared after the phylloxera, but has made a comeback because it botrytises easily on well-ventilated sites (although it does not like wet weather) and has fine acids and smooth flavours. Kövérszőlő, which has potential as a varietal wine, can be recognised by its large, elongated berries.

KABAR (until recently known by its research name of Tarcal 10) is an early-ripening cross of Bouvier with Hárslevelű. Its smaller berries produce less (but more-concentrated) juice. Much of the development work was carried out at Dereszla Winery, where the 2006 vintage produced a sound wine with marked Hárslevelű characteristics. As yet little has been planted while vintners assess its potential.

THE RANGE OF TOKAJI WINES

MOST ATTENTION has been focused on the Aszú wines because they first made Tokaj famous. However, Tokaji soils produce great wines in many different styles. It may be that in the future Tokaji will become equally well-known for its dry and off-dry wines.

DRY AND SEMIDRY VARIETAL WINES – Regional vintners have always produced dry and semidry wines for domestic consumption. However, those made up to the early '90s excited very little interest beyond the

boundaries of Tokaji. But in 2000 Király-udvar made a truly sumptuous dry Furmint from an exceptional crop of very ripe but unbotrytised grapes from the upper part of the stony Úrágya Vineyard. The wine was fermented and matured in wood and had the richness of flavour, concentration and complexity of a great white wine.

As a result of this success other leading wineries started producing top-quality dry Furmints. Today this classy, food-friendly variety is attracting more serious attention.

Winemakers have also turned their attention beyond Furmint to Hárslevelű and Yellow Muscat. The former produces crisp, fruity semidry wines; the latter wonderfully aromatic wines with fine acids.

Szamorodni – This name is Polish for 'as it comes' and refers to the fact that grapes picked for this style of wine are in bunches with a variable percentage of botrytised and non-botrytised grapes.

The bunches are pressed and the juice macerated with the skins before being lightly pressed again, fermented, and matured in wood for at least two years. The wine has a marked raisin taste with a rich nutty flavour.

In some years when there is less sugar in the grapes, they are left to ferment completely, leaving no residual sugar. The resultant dry wine is then racked into casks that are not completely filled, to allow a thin film of yeasty growth called flor to float on top of the wine. This process enriches the flavours and endows the wine with its nutty, sherry-like character.

Dry Szamorodni is a difficult style to make well, and it requires subtlety to tease out its exquisite walnut flavours. However, the reward is a growing appreciation of this aperitif style by gourmets and the restaurant trade.

Thus there are two styles of Szamorodni – *édes* ('sweet') and *száraz* ('dry') – that are both less expensive than Aszú wines (because their harvesting is less labour-intensive), and both deserve attention in their own right.

LATE-HARVEST CUVEES – This style originally known as *főbor* ('prime') was reintroduced in 1995. István Szepsy was in the vanguard of the movement by Tokaji winemakers determined to produce a lighter style of Tokaj wine for contemporary oenophiles.

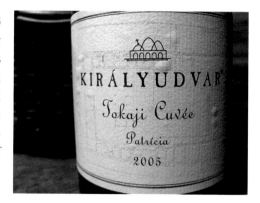

BOTRYTISED grapes are picked in bunches as for Szamorodni. However, for the főbor they are macerated in fresh must, pressed gently and fermented quickly. Any secondary fermentation is stopped by cooling, and the wine is racked into cask for six months before being bottled. A further six or seven months of bottle-ageing means that the wine can be released some 12-14 months or so after the harvest with a delightfully fresh and fruity flavour.

THERE IS ALSO GROWING interest in superbly crafted late-harvest varietal wines made from the three most widely planted varieties – Furmint, Hárslevelű, and Yellow Muscat.

MÁSLÁS AND FORDÍTÁS – These two other older styles, made from second or third pressings of Aszú berries, have retained a local following because they are popularly priced. However, they are rarely seen outside Tokaj.

ASZÚ – In our brief history section we showed how Aszús evolved from the eastern Mediterranean countries and were refined in Tokaj. What sets Tokaji Aszú apart from other great late-harvest wines is the mineral nature of the soil and the extraordinary set of climatic conditions that nature has assembled in Tokaji to generate botrytis, and to balance sugar with natural acidity.

HOWEVER, because the degree of botrytisation varies with each harvest according to the weather, a grading system was introduced to indicate the degree of residual sugar in the wine when it is bottled. Thus on a Tokaji Aszú wine label you will find a number between 3 and 6 followed by the word *puttonyos* (the traditional wooden harvesting hod), which denotes the number of puttony of aszú berries mixed with the base wine in a 136-litre barrel. The table below sets out the amount of residual sugar required to comply with the Tokaji Wine Board's law for Aszú wines from 3 to 6 puttonyos, Aszú-Eszencia and Essencia. Aszú wines must also have the listed minimum levels of dry extract and at least 7g/l tartaric acid.

puttonyos	grams/litre sugar	grams/litre dry extract
3	60-90	25
4	90-120	30
5	120-150	35
6	150-180	40
Aszú-Eszencia	over 180	45
Essencia	over 240	50

ASZÚ 6-PUTTONYOS and Aszú-Eszencia are sought-after because of their complexity and longevity. However, we believe that all well-made Aszú wines have something to offer the enthusiast. The 3-puttonyos wines have fruit and flavour, organoleptic sensitivity is heightened in the 4-puttonyos, while greater richness is evident in the 5-puttonyos.

IN OUTSTANDING VINTAGE years 5- or 6-puttonyos Aszú wines are made from single vineyards, and in some cases from single varieties. Some of the best that we have tasted that are still available from wine merchants specialising in Tokaji wines include: Szarvas 1994 (Crown Estates), Mézes Mály 1999 (Royal Tokaj), Kapi 1999 (Disznókő), Lapis 1999 (Királyudvar), Chateau Pajzos 1999, Nyulászó 1999 (Royal Tokaj), Hétszőlő 1999, and Bendecz 2000 (Patricius). Of the single-variety wines we would point out the Aszú 6-Puttonyos Hárslevelű 1999 from Árvay, and the Aszú 5-Puttonyos Hárslevelű 1999 from Hétszőlő.

TOKAJ ESSENCIA – Tokaj Essencia is the highest category of all. It is the most concentrated you can get, being the first-run juice that flows from the botrytised grapes when they are brought to the winery. Essencia will often have around 800 grams/litre of residual sugar. Such a concentration of sugar means that fermentation is slow and rarely produces a wine of more than five degrees of alcohol. It is fermented in demijohns and transferred to small barrels to be aged for ten or more years before bottling.

ESSENCIA IS PURE NECTAR. Its legendary healing and restorative powers made it a favourite with European monarchs. Bottles were offered as royal gifts on par with jewels and precious metals.

MADAME DE POMPADOUR is said to have encouraged Louis XIV to enjoy Essencia, and King Gustav III of Sweden drank little else. Napoleon III ordered Tokaji Essencia every year that it was made, and Peter the Great, Catherine the Great, and Frederick the Great all treasured it. Beethoven and Liszt rhapsodized it, and Goethe and Voltaire sang its praises as a remarkable wine that enlivened body and soul.

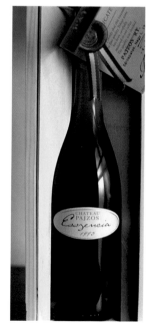

THE BEST VINTAGES of Tokaj Essencia can cost around Ft 120,000 or more per 50cl bottle. If you are ever offered the chance to taste a sip, accept this fortuitous opportunity whether you like sweet wines or not. It is an experience you are unlikely to forget.

THE MOST OUTSTANDING Tokaji Essencia wines we have tasted that are still available include: 1993 Chateau Pajzos, 1993 Disznókő, 1999 István Szepsy, 1999 Royal Tokaj, and 2000 Pendits.

TOKAJ VINTAGES

THIS SHORT SUMMARY of recent Tokaji vintages starts with the great 1993 vintage, which was the first for many of the newly refurbished wineries after privatisation. Prior to 1993 the most remarkable vintages of the 20th century were 1900, 1906, 1912, 1915, 1920, 1936, 1937, 1947, 1956, 1963, 1964, 1972, 1983 and 1988.

1993 Exceptional year with many outstanding Aszú wines.

1994 A poor year, although the Great Growth Szarvas Vineyard produced a very fine Aszú 6-puttonyos.

1995 A very good year just falling short of excellent.

1996 Late summer rains made the season difficult, but good weather in November saved the vintage for those growers brave enough to delay harvesting until then.

1997 The dry autumn restricted botrytisation, hence a small harvest but one which produced some fine wines.

1998 Rain spoiled the harvest. The wines had little character.

1999 One of the great vintages of the century – excellent botrytisation, very fine acids, superb wines.

2000 Another classic year yielding very ripe grapes with high sugar content.

2001 Promised well, but in the end rain spoiled the vintage.

2002 Again the vintage looked promising until rain came, although some excellent wines were made from grapes picked in September.

2003 A long harvest starting at the end of August and continuing into late November. Dryness restricted the amount of botrytisation, yet produced complex wines with fine aromas.

2004 A cool and damp growing season. Few 6-puttonyos wines were made but the 3-, 4-, and 5-puttonyos wines were elegant and gracious.

2005 A long Indian summer provided excellent-quality grapes. Exceptional Aszú wines were made with great flavours. A very good vintage.

2006 Early indications are that the harvest of aszú berries was small but of a very good quality.

MATCHING TOKAJI WINES WITH FOOD

MANY OF HUNGARY'S BEST CHEFS, as well as many in leading international restaurants, have been devising new dishes to match the different Tokaji wine styles. There are some excellent food-and-wine-matching recipe books on the market, such as those produced by Gundel and Gabriella Mészáros. However, rather than list a lot of different recipes we thought it might be more useful to pass on some of the basic ground rules for matching Tokaji wines with food.

THE BEST DRY FURMINTS are strong wines with a steely background reflecting the mineral nature of the soil. Seafood, caviar, fish without strong flavouring, grilled meat served with compote of quince, and even wild poultry marry well with such wines, chilled to 10°C.

DRY SZAMORODNI makes an excellent aperitif, but is also in perfect harmony with Hungarian pork dishes and stuffed cabbage.

HÁRSLEVELŰ is more delicate: it has less forceful acids and a delightful honey-like aroma. It is better-suited to non-acidic foods, such as whitefish without strong flavouring.

LATE-HARVEST WINES, often labelled as Cuvees, are young, fresh and rich, and they can support more acidic dishes or ingredients. Goose and duck liver containing both fats and sugars are ideal, preferably without garlic and onion. Goat cheese, seafood dishes with creamy sauces, and poultry with fruit make happy accompaniments.

THE FINEST ASZÚ WINES with expansive aromas and layers of taste will require richer foods, such as roasted goose with a rich chestnut sauce, to show them at their best. Duck with peaches or venison with sweet fruit sauce and fresh spring vegetables also work well, as do Chinese sweet-and-sour dishes.

MANY ASZÚ enthusiasts believe that a creamy Roquefort cheese is a perfect match with the richer Aszús. Others prefer mature ewe's cheese. White peaches, ripe apricots, peach and apricot flans, sponge cake and chocolate fondue are just some of the desserts that show off Aszú flavours.

AND FOR AFTER DINING, we are reliably informed that the complex flavours of old Aszú wines are accentuated with a fine Havana cigar.

SERVING WINE

WE ASKED KÁLMÁN KOZMA, chairman of the Hungarian Sommelier Association and a director of Budapest's famed Gundel Restaurant, for some advice about serving wine. He confirmed that taking care in the preparation and serving of Tokaji wines pays handsome dividends.

KOZMA SUGGESTS that the lighter, dry wines are best served fresh but not too cold – around 7°C, with the stronger dry Furmints at around 10°C.

DRY AND SWEET SZAMORODNI and late-harvest wines are agreeable at 12°C (or even a degree or two cooler) but the richer Aszú wines are better served at 12-14°C in order to allow their aromas to develop. Some gourmets even like them at room temperature.

GLASSES can make a huge difference to the taste of wine. The finer the wine the more important it is to select the right glass.

MOST FRUIT-DRIVEN WINES have pleasing aromas. By pouring a little at a time – less than third of a good-sized glass – the recipient can swirl the glass without spillage. Nosing the bouquet is very much part of the enjoyment of drinking wine.

SHOULD THE FINEST ASZÚ WINES be served in a larger or smaller glass? We consider it to be entirely a matter of personal preference. Smaller tulip-shaped glasses, or even slim white-wine glasses, look extremely elegant – but it seems sensible to have a glass large enough to explore the wine because older Aszús offer many intriguing aromas that continue to develop in the glass for some time after pouring.

The Touring

TRAVELLING TO AND AROUND TOKAJ

MOST NATIONAL CARRIERS and many budget airlines use Budapest International Airport (BUD) at Ferihegy, some 24 kilometres southeast of Budapest, which offers fixed-price taxi and minibus services into the city centre. The airport minibus brings passengers directly to their destination address and charges around Ft 2,500 one-way; the taxi service costs approximately Ft 4,000. Taxis can be pre-booked; see www.zonataxi.eu for details.

THE BEST DIRECT TRAIN service to Tokaj leaves Budapest's Keleti (East) Station at 7:35, 9:35, and 11:35 each morning. The journey is scheduled to take two hours and 35 minutes, and return fare is about Ft 5,500. Train times can be checked on www.elvira.hu, which also gives information on rail travel to other towns in the region. The train station at Tokaj is about one kilometre from the town centre; there is an hourly bus available and a local taxi service.

THERE ARE MANY international car-rental firms at Budapest Airport and in the city that offer all-inclusive rates. Some agencies such as Fox Autorent (www.foxautorent.com) will deliver a car to your Budapest hotel. If you drive on motorways in Hungary you will need to prepay for a motorway pass; ask the rental agency to obtain one for you. If you prefer to get your own pass from a petrol station en route to the motorway, remember there can be long queues at weekends.

THE ROAD TO TOKAJ is straightforward. From the centre of Budapest, head up Andrássy út through Heroes' Square, following signs to the

M3 Motorway towards Miskolc. Take M40 (E71) around Miskolc before turning left onto Road 37 in the direction of Sátoraljaújhely through Szerencs.

BUS TRAVEL WITHIN TOKAJI is scarce and infrequent. There are frequent trains from Tokaj to Sárospatak. For local travel information we advise checking with Tourinform's Tokaj office (T: +36 47 352 259).

PLANNING YOUR TRIP

ONCE YOU HAVE DECIDED the length of your visit we suggest that you make appointments with the wineries that you most want to visit. When booking visits and tastings with wineries check on costs, timings and languages spoken. Winery tours and tasting usually last one and a half hours.

THE NEXT STEP is to book accommodation and dining arrangements by e-mail, fax or telephone, asking for confirmation of the booking, room rates, directions and languages spoken. English and German is increasingly spoken in hotels and restaurants.

VISITING WINERIES

MANY OF THE LARGER WINERIES are members of the Tokaj Renaissance Association, an organisation dedicated to restoring the reputation of Tokaji wines by encouraging producers to work to the highest standards.

THESE WINERIES generally have very good visitor facilities and we have provided some basic information about them. Information about smaller family wineries (many of whom make excellent wines) is more limited and in some cases we can only provide a thumbnail sketch.

PLEASE BEAR in mind that in smaller family-run businesses, the owners tend to be out working in the vineyard or cellar. Wherever possible we recommend making contact in advance by e-mail or fax, otherwise telephone in the early evening. It is worthwhile taking the trouble to make sure they can receive you, and that you can understand them.

IT IS NORMAL PRACTICE for wineries to charge visitors for a tour and tasting. In some of the smaller wineries, where they do not request a fee, it is appreciated if you buy a couple of bottles before leaving. If you are travelling by car, remember that it is illegal to drive after consuming any alcohol at all, so be sure to expectorate when tasting or plan accordingly.

WE RECOMMEND that you carry a small notebook and pencil to write down your preferred wines – and also difficult-to-pronounce Hungarian names when asking for directions, such as Pendits (pronounced 'pen ditch') at Abaújszántó (pronounced 'a boy santo').

IT IS ALSO A GOOD IDEA to carry a light jacket or sweater with you if you plan to go down into deep cool cellars. Even on the warmest summer days the cellar temperature remains constant at 10°C.

FOR EASE of reference all those wineries we mention in the companion are listed in the index under 'Wineries'.

VINEYARDS

OUR MAPS SHOW THE LOCATIONS of Tokaji's greatest vineyards. You will find them listed under 'Vineyards' in the index. We give some basic information about them on the pages devoted to the wineries with which they have a particular association. For example, information about the Great Growth Szarvas is shown under Crown Estates.

WHEN YOU VISIT vineyards please remember that they are private property, and visitors should not pick fruit nor disturb the vines in any way. The great advantage of walking on paths through or around vineyards is to experience the microclimate and see for yourself the different soils, grape varieties and viticultural methods practised.

ATTRACTIONS

IN MOST AREAS we have listed activities other than visiting wineries. Museums, nature or hiking trails, river trips and more are listed in the index. The Tourinform offices in Tokaj and Sárospatak are useful sources of further information.

HOTELS AND RESTAURANTS

OUR LISTINGS of accommodations and dining facilities for each area is selective rather than exhaustive. In spring of 2007 we tried and tested all places recommended to stay or eat. Hotel, *panzió* (Hungarian for 'guesthouses'), and bed-and-breakfast establishments are listed under 'Accommodations'; restaurants and other eateries under 'Dining'. Telephone, e-mail, and Website details are given when available.

TOKAJI IS A REGION where it is normally quite easy to find clean, comfortable bed-and-breakfast accommodation at a cost between Ft 5,000-10,000 per night. However, if you plan to travel during the main Tokaji festivals, we strongly advise making bookings in advance and asking for confirmation of the booking and room rate. Tokaj's main spring and autumn festivals generally take place in May and October; dates vary from year to year, so consult www.tokaj.hu before booking. If you want to stay in a particular hotel it is best to book directly with them.

WE RECOMMEND MAKING reservations for all popular restaurants. More often than not, your host hotel or panzio will make local telephone reservations on your behalf.

MOST RESTAURANTS offer set menus for a good value and sell a comprehensive range of wines by the glass. The price of wine is normally quoted per decilitre. This practice allows the visitor to sample several wines at a very reasonable cost. However, please remember that it is illegal to drive in Hungary after consuming any alcohol whatsoever.

IN MORE MODEST EATING establishments it is always best to ask about the dish of the day or local specialities that are readily available. In such places the wine selection may be rather more limited but you will find that most local and regional wines are well-made and generally sensibly priced. Bottled water is universally available.

FOOD AND WINE SHOPPING IN TOKAJ

THERE IS ALWAYS SOMETHING special about bringing home a bottle or two of wine from a winery one has visited, having possibly met the vintner.

MANY OF THE TOKAJI WINERIES have shops (often called vinotechs) where wines, wine books, and wine maps may be purchased. Because of weight restrictions imposed by most airlines it makes sense to select special bottles of 3-, 4-, 5-, or 6-puttonyos Aszú wines which are sold in 50cl bottles. Dry and sweet Szamorodnis and late-harvest cuvees are also sold in 50cl bottles.

THERE ARE FEW UNIQUE REGIONAL FOODS, but we would like to draw your attention to the cheeses that can be tasted with Tokaji. Dobogó, the Zwack Family winery in the heart of Tokaj town, has a South Tyrolean blue cheese made with Tokaji grapes that is a perfect match for its late-harvest and Aszú wines.

DRY, SUNNY WINE-PRODUCING REGIONS such as Tokaji are suited to rearing goats, and many gourmets claim that there is nothing quite like fresh or mature goat's-milk cheese to bring out the best qualities of Tokaji Aszús.

THERE IS AN OUTSTANDING biodynamic goat-cheese maker near Károlyfalvay, in the Zemplén Hills before Sátoraljaújhely. Simply known as Enikő, she makes her cheeses under exacting conditions from the fresh milk of her properly-fed, healthy goats. Enikő's cheeses can be tasted in several local wineries such as Hudacskó in Bodrogkisfalud, as well as in Ős Kaján and other discerning restaurants.

SUGGESTED ITINERARIES

WE HAVE TAKEN THE LIBERTY of suggesting two itineraries for first-time visitors: the first for those coming on a weekend visit by train, the second for those coming by car for a week-long stay.

WEEKEND VISIT BY TRAIN
Day 1

7:35	Depart Budapest's Keleti (East) Station (rail tickets should be booked in advance)
10:11	Arrive Tokaj, take taxi or 20-minute walk to Kossuth tér in the centre of Tokaj
11:00	Hétszőlő's Rákóczi Cellars
12:30	Lunch
14:00	Árvay Winery
15:30	Dobogó Winery
17:00	Hímesudvar Winery
18:00	Tokaj town sightseeing

Day 2

10:00	Tokaj Museum
11:00	Demeter Winery
11:30	Erzsébet Winery
13:00	Lunch
15:30	Bott Winery
17:50	Depart Tokaj
20:27	Arrive Budapest

WEEK-LONG VISIT BY CAR
Day 1

8:00	Depart Budapest
11:00	Disznókő Winery
12:30	Lunch at Sárga Borház at Disznókő Winery
14:30	Royal Tokaj Winery in Mád
16:00	Úri Borok Winery, Tokaj Classic Winery, or Gábor Orosz Winery in Mád
19:30	Dinner at Mádi Kúria with Gundel wines

Day 2

9:00	Walk in the vineyards around Szent Tamás Hill
10:00	30-minute drive to Pendits Winery in Abaújszántó
12:00	30-minute drive to Mihály Hollókői Winery in Tállya
12:30	Lunch at Hollókői Winery restaurant
14:00	30-minute drive through the Zemplén Hills to Erdőbénye
14:30	Vivamus Winery in Erdőbénye
16:30	Attila Homonna Winery in Erdőbénye
19:30	Dinner at Ős Kaján Restaurant in Tolcsva

Day 3

10:00	Béres Winery in Erdőbénye
11:30	Patricius Winery near Szegi
13:00	Lunch at Magita Hotel
14:30	20-minute drive to Tolcsva
15:00	Oremus Winery
16:30	20-minute drive to Sárospatak
19:30	Dinner at Vár Vendéglő

Day 4

10:00	Visit Sárospatak Castle
11:00	Rákóczi Cellars at Sárospatak Castle
12:30	30-minute drive to Sátoraljaújhely, passing by the Oremus Vineyard, return to Sárospatak
15:00	Evinor Winery in Sárospatak
16:00	Sárospatak town sightseeing

Day 5

9:30	20-minute drive to Bodrogkeresztúr
10:00	Dereszla Winery
11:30	Hudacskó Winery, Puklus Winery, Füleky Winery, or Tokaj Nobilis Winery
13:00	20-minute drive to Tokaj
13:30	Lunch
14:30	Hétszőlő Rákóczi Cellars
16:00	Dobogó Winery
19:30	Dinner at Dégenfeld Palace

Day 6

10:00	Árvay Winery
11:30	Tokaj Museum
12:30	Lunch
14:00	Zoltán Demeter Winery
15:30	Hímesudvar Winery or Erzsébet Winery
17:00	20-minute drive to Tarcal passing Hétszőlő and Szarvas vineyards
19:30	Dinner at Dégenfeld Castle Hotel or Andrássy Hotel

Day 7

9:00	Walk or drive up St. Terézia Hill, passing Johnson's Var in Mézes Mály Vineyard
10:00	Dégenfeld Winery
11:30	Andrássy Winery
13:00	Lunch
14:30	Kikelet Winery, Tokajicum Winery, or Dorogi Winery
16:00	Return to Budapest

The Essentials

MAPS

THE MAPS FOR EACH AREA show the main roads and the locations of the larger wineries, notable vineyards, hotels, and restaurants. Look under 'Maps' in the index to find their page numbers.

MONEY

THE FORINT (Ft or HUF) is Hungary's official unit of currency. Banknotes are issued in denominations of 200, 500, 1,000, 2,000, 5,000, 10,000, and 20,000 bills. Most hotels and restaurants, wine shops, travel offices and stores accept major credit cards. However, if you are using bed-and-breakfast establishments, smaller local restaurants, and public services you will need to carry forints.

IN BUDAPEST there is a profusion of bank machines. However, outside the capital you will find them more widely dispersed. Towns such as Tokaj and Sárospatak feature cash points but you are unlikely to find them in small towns and villages.

CHECK THE CURRENT exchange rates at banks. As of October 2007 the exchange rates were roughly Ft 350 = £1UK, Ft 200 = $1US, and Ft 250 = €1EURO. Where we quote prices they are in Hungarian forints.

WEIGHTS AND MEASURES

WEIGHTS AND MEASURES are normally metric. Sugar, acid and dry extract levels are all measured in grams per litre (g/l). We give distances in kilometres (km) because Hungarian maps and signposts display them; a kilometre equals 0.625 miles. We also follow the local practice of stating the size of vineyard estates in hectares; one hectare equals 2.48 acres.

NAMES AND SPELLINGS

WE USE THE HUNGARIAN SPELLINGS of towns and places because these are the names that are signposted in the region. We often refer to wineries by their simple names, such as Oremus rather than Tokaj Oremus, its official name.

THE SPELLING of the word Tokaj varies from country to country. In England it has long been spelt 'Tokay', but we use Tokaj for the town and Tokaji for the region. Tokaji also means 'of Tokaj', as in Tokaji Aszú, meaning Aszú wines from the town or region of Tokaj.

WHEREVER WE CAN, we give the etymological meaning of place names because they usually refer to a local geographical feature, flora or fauna, or notable Hungarians. For example Várhegy means 'castle hill', Szarvas means 'deer', and Rákóczi was the family name of the ruling princes of Transylvania in the 17th century. Hungarians normally give their surname first, for example Rákóczi György (whereas we would say George Rákóczi). We have maintained the English style throughout to avoid confusion.

THERE ARE VARIOUS SPELLINGS of some place names and words, such as the term 'essencia' – the traditional spelling for the wine that is the pure essence of aszú grapes. However, you will also come across 'Aszú-Eszencia' where one 's' becomes a 'z'. This is to distinguish the wine that is an extension to the Aszú range from the highly concentrated first-run juice – the absolute essence – that is drawn off first and vinified quite separately.

TELEPHONE COMMUNICATION

TO TELEPHONE HUNGARY from outside the country, use the '00' international access code, wait for the change of dial tone, then dial country code '36', followed by the required number. Areas within Hungary (except Budapest) have a two-digit code: for Tokaj it is '47'. Telephone numbers outside Budapest have six digits. Thus to contact Tourinform Tokaj from outside Hungary, dial '00 36 47 352 259'.

THE AREA CODE for Budapest is '1', and Budapest telephone numbers are seven digits long (excluding the country code). Within Budapest local calls can be made by dialling the seven-digit number only.

WHEN MAKING CALLS within Hungary, the inter-area code is '06'. Thus to call Tourinform Tokaj from Budapest, dial '06 47 352 259'.

THE THREE CELL-PHONE PROVIDERS in Hungary are T-Mobile, Pannon, and Vodafone. To call a land-line from a cell-phone you need the inter-area code '06' followed by the area code and number.

MOST PUBLIC TELEPHONES in Hungary are operated by phone cards which can be purchased from post offices, newsstands, tourist offices and some hotels. There are coin-operated boxes that take Ft 20, 50, and 100 pieces, but be warned – some of them have a nasty habit of swallowing coins all too quickly.

USEFUL WEBSITES

www.tokaj.hu – Comprehensive Tokaj information
www.tourinform.hu – General Hungary tourism information
www.tokaji.hu – Tokaj Renaissance Association homepage
www.bud.hu – Budapest Airport information
www.elvira.hu – Hungarian railway timetables
www.malev.hu – Hungarian national airline homepage

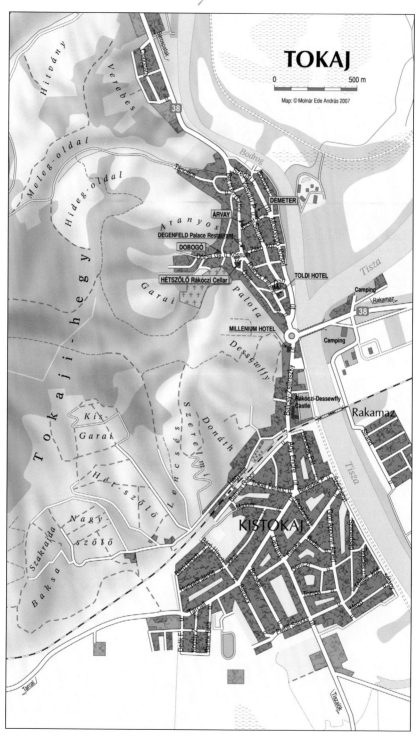

Tokaj Hill

THE TOKAJ HILL AREA includes the small towns of Tokaj, Tarcal, Bodrogkeresztúr and Bodrogkisfalud, all of which nestle around the 512-metre-high hill that dominates the region.

THE BEDROCK of the hill is andesite, rhyolite and rhyolitic tuff. It is covered with a very thick layer of loess – twenty or more metres deep – that imparts a honey-rich flavour to the wines.

TOKAJ TOWN is a good place to start our tour, not only because it gave its name to the region but also because of its geographic and historical significance. It was a major crossing point on the upper Tisza River, and from the 12th to the 17th centuries Tokaj boasted a castle on the island at the Tisza's confluence with the Bodrog River. Tokaj gained in commercial importance by being at the crossroads of the north-south and east-west trade routes. Transylvanian salt and then Tokaji wine became major commodities with northern Europe, providing Tokaj with a connection to the world that continues today.

ATTRACTIONS

THE NEWLY-RENOVATED TOURINFORM visitor centre at Serház utca 1 (on the corner at Rákóczi utca, opposite Murphys Bar) is a useful first port of call to gather local travel information and maps. (T: +36 47 552 070, F: +36 47 352 259; tokaj@tourinform.hu)

THE TOKAJ MUSEUM is housed in the former residence of a wealthy Greek merchant at Gábor Bethlen utca 7 – a minute's walk from Kossuth tér. The building is a reminder of the golden age of Tokaj when Greek traders transformed the townscape by constructing two- and three-story houses with gar-

dens, inspired by fine architectural design. Hitherto, estate managers, workers, and local artisans lived in simple single-story houses while the aristocracy resided in splendid countryside manors.

THE MUSEUM has some fine exhibits of period furniture, wall paintings, and dress and travel accessories. However, the most interesting exhibits for the bibulous traveller are to be found on the top floor, where a collection of old winemaking and cooperage tools is displayed. There is a well-preserved haulier's cart laden with gönci barrels (the traditional Tokaji 136-litre barrel made in the Zemplén Hills village of Gönc). Such carts needed to be well-made to carry their precious cargo on the long journeys north to Poland and Russia.

THERE IS ALSO AN INTRIGUING COLLECTION of old wine labels. One for Chateau Windischgraetz Aszú is a reminder that Tokaj had an established Bordeaux-style domain system in the 19th century; another is a very stylish label for a Tokaji Sec, suggesting that quality dry wines are not a new thing in Tokaj; a third label for Tokaj Asszu (sic) reveals that other spellings of Aszú were used.

DOWN IN THE CELLAR, samples of the main Tokaji vineyard soil types – clay, loess and nyirok – are displayed, and the traditional method of stake training is also shown.

THE MUSEUM is well-worth visiting for an hour or so and the Ft 600 admission charge allows use of the pleasant little garden for a rest.

ONE BLOCK down from the Museum is the Tokaj Conference Centre, which was once the town's synagogue. Many Jewish traders settled in the town and made a substantial contribution to the exports of Tokaj wines. When the Jewish population swelled to a thousand they built a large synagogue. Sadly, in 1944 the entire Jewish population was roughly rounded up and taken to Nazi death camps. Only 100 ever returned, and in the difficult postwar years the synagogue fell into disrepair.

NOW COMPLETELY RENOVATED, it serves as a modern conference centre and concert hall, and there are plans to add a 300-seat theatre and community centre on an adjoining site to enable Tokaj to stage events that will develop civic life and prolong the summer tourist season.

WE RECOMMEND DRIVING or walking to the top of Tokaj Hill, locally known as Bald Mountain. On a clear day your reward will be panoramic views of the Great Hungarian Plain and the Bodrog and Tisza flood plains. It is the combination of the great heat from the plain and the cool waters of the rivers that creates the misty conditions for noble rot to produce aszú berries.

TO DRIVE up the hill you will need to go into the centre of Tarcal and turn right at the signpost to the TV mast, and follow the winding service road to the top of the hill – about a 25-minute drive from Tokaj. To make the ascent on foot from the Tokaj town centre, head up Dózsa György utca through the cemetery on to a well-trodden path that joins a wider track after about 300 metres. Turn right along the track up a short incline and look for the left turn onto a spur leading to the top of the hill, easily identified by the tall TV tower. A gentle walk with frequent stops will take about an hour and a half.

THE VOLCANIC BEDROCK and loess topsoil of the hill are home to a surprising range of flora and fauna, although much of the original native vegetation on the lower south-facing slopes has been replaced by vineyards.

HOWEVER, MANY PROTECTED species have survived on the higher slopes, where you will find the Pannonian white oak and the manna, a low tree with twisted branches that looks as if it has had a bad-hair day.

SPRING IS A WONDERFUL TIME to see feather-grass, yellow Adonis, and the Hungarian iris – a botanical rarity – in bloom. There is also a wide range of wild orchids to be seen: species with unusual names such as Toothed, Greater Butterfly, Frog, and Lizard.

IN SUMMER THE SNOWDROP windflower opens, soon to be followed by a profusion of European Michaelmas daisies. The so-called Bald Mountain nurtures some 20 other rare plants.

ACCOMMODATIONS IN TOKAJ

TOLDI FOGADÓ

A pleasant, newly-opened (2006) three-star hotel and restaurant featuring 20 air-conditioned rooms with private bathrooms that describes itself as a "5-puttonyos wellness house." There is an indoor swimming pool, sauna, massage

facilities, and an outdoor beer garden. The hotel restaurant is air-conditioned and there is a cosy bar. Avoid being tempted by the offer of rooms with a river view, because they also overlook the Tokaj bypass that is often busy with heavy-goods traffic heading up to the Slovakian border.

> **Toldi Fogadó**
> 3910 Tokaj, Hajdú köz 2
> T: +36 47 353 403
> F: +36 47 353 402
> info@toldifogado.hu
> www.toldifogado.hu

MILLENNIUM HOTEL

> **Millennium Hotel**
> Bajcsy-Zsilinszky utca 34
> T: +36 47 352 247
> millennium@axelero.hu

Well-located opposite the Dessewffy Mansion, the hotel has 18 spacious and reasonably priced double rooms. The hotel offers free Internet connection and the room rate includes a buffet breakfast. The hotel has its own restaurant and also offers small conference facilities.

> **Makk Marci Panzió**
> 3910 Tokaj, Liget köz 1
> T: +36 47 352 336
> F: +36 47 353 088
> makkmarci@axelero.hu

MAKK MARCI PANZIÓ

Easily found opposite Tokaj's post office, this panzió is spotlessly clean and comfortable, and the room rate includes a hearty breakfast. Freshly cooked pizzas are available from 10:00-22:00 daily.

DÉGENFELD PALACE

The title 'Palace' is a bit misleading – although the building was originally a fine old townhouse belonging to Count Dégenfeld, it has been converted into a business conference facility and has only four comfortable but straightforward bedrooms. The real advantage of these rooms for the

bibulous traveller is that they are upstairs from an excellent provincial restaurant. Rooms are let at reasonable rates, though breakfasts are extra – but unless you are on a very tight budget, don't hesitate to order the morning meals, as they're luxurious and will set you up for the day.

> **Dégenfeld Palace**
> 3910 Tokaj, Kossuth tér 1
> T: +36 47 552 173
> F: +36 47 552 174
> palota@degenfeld.hu
> www.tokajtc.com

ERZSÉBET PANZIÓ

> **Erzsébet Panzió**
> 3910 Tokaj, Bem utca 16
> T: +36 47 353 549
> M: +36 20 9259 931
> info@erzsebetpince.hu
> www.erzsebetpince.hu

From Kossuth Square follow Bem utca round the top of town to find the panzió on the left. It has two well-furnished rooms above the cellars that housed Czarina Elisabeth's Tokaji wine purchases before they were carried home to Russia. Close to the centre of Tokaj, Erzsébet Panzió is within easy walking distance of all the town's wineries and main attractions.

DINING IN TOKAJ

DÉGENFELD PALACE

A spacious, well-appointed restaurant where one can dine sumptuously at reasonable cost, located on Kossuth tér opposite the Catholic Church and Rákóczi Cellars. In summer there are tables outside on the main

> **Dégenfeld Palace**
> Tokaj, Kossuth tér 1
> T: +36 47 552 173
> palota@degenfeld.hu
> www.tokajtc.hu

square. The menu offers excellent food-and-wine matches, and the owners have an enlightened policy of listing other producers' wines as well as their own.

BONCHIDAI CSÁRDA

A few paces down from the bridge on the left-hand side of Bajcsy-Zsilinszky lies this good-sized country inn overlooking the Bodrog River and handily placed next to the riverboat terminal. The food is rustic but a good value. The fish soups and their speciality catfish dish are worthy of your attention.

Bonchidai Csárda
Bajcsy-Zsilinszky utca 21
T: +36 47 352 632

TAVERNA RESTAURANT

By the bridge at the confluence of the two rivers, this is a relatively new restaurant where English is spoken, serving popular food at reasonable prices.

Taverna Restaurant
3910 Tokaj, Hősök tere 1
T: +36 47 352 346
info@tokajtaverna.hu
www.tokajtaverna.hu

The Toldi and Millennium hotels (see above) also have good restaurants. Information can be gained from their websites given above. We can also recommend the pizzeria on Kossuth tér.

WINERIES

ÁRVAY ÉS TÁRSA

FROM 1992-2000, János Árvay was the chief winemaker at Disznókő, where he was part of the team that produced a series of outstanding wines that have become recognised as the new face of Tokaj.

HOWEVER, LIKE OTHER GREAT WINE-MAKERS who harbour a deep love for their land, Árvay's true ambition was to develop his own family winery. He found a wonderful partner

Árvay és Társa
3910 Tokaj, József Attila utca 2
T: +36 47 374 025
F: +36 47 552 156
tokaj.hetfurtos@axelero.hu
www.arvaybor.hu
Directions: 200 metres down Gábor Bethlen utca from Kossuth tér. The entrance is on József Attila utca.
Owner: János Árvay and Partner
Estate: 120ha; 83ha under vine in 18 locations in the Mád Basin and on Tokaj Hill. New plantings have been made at a density of 5,500 vines per hectare on a medium cordon; old stake-plantings at a density of 10,000 vines per hectare.
Tour and tasting cost: Ft 2,500
Visiting hours: 10:00-17:00
Languages spoken: English, Hungarian

in Christian Sauska, a Hungarian based in the USA who has helped him create a 120-hectare estate, two-thirds of which is currently under vine.

IT IS NOT a homogeneous estate like Disznókő, but is made up of 18 different plots in different types of soil, allowing Árvay to select his wines for blending from a wide spectrum of flavours.

A STRICT VINICULTURIST, Árvay prunes back to seven bunches per vine, hence his adoption of the brand name Hétfürtös, which in Hungarian means 'seven bunches'. Wherever possible he purchased stake-planted vineyards with old Furmint and Hárslevelű vines; he still prefers to use stake-planting, particularly on the steeper slopes of vineyards.

HIS BLENDS ARE BASED ON THE FURMINT, Hárslevelű, and Yellow Muscat that provide the structure, aroma, and richness of taste that he likes in his wines. His aim is to make pure, fresh wines that show off their natural fruit flavours, such as his late-harvest Édes Élet ('Sweet Life'), the wine that he first made as a surprise for his partner's wedding in 2002.

WHEN VOTED WINEMAKER of the Year in 2003, Árvay attributed his success to hard work in the vineyard and a constant desire to experiment and develop wines for different moods and occasions.

WE CAN VOUCH for his special relationship with his vineyard workers and his deep love for his land, whether he is on the steep slopes of the Szerelmi overlooking Tokaj town or on the more gentle inclines of Istenhegy near his home in Rátka village, where he was born and bred.

ÁRVAY RUNS THE BUSINESS with his daughter Angelika, whose knowledge of wine, marketing skills, and fluent English make her an essential partner in the close-knit Árvay team.

Range of Wines

DRY FURMINT ISTENHEGY 2003 Bone-dry and vibrant single-vineyard wine with good fruit and fine acids. A food-friendly wine with a soft pear aroma and ripe fruit to delight the palate.

VULCANUS Named after the Roman god of fire, this late-harvest wine has the minerality that is a reminder of the character of the Tokaji terroir. Its dry finish will delight gourmet palates.

CASINO CUVEE 2000 A stylish late-harvest wine with the residual sugar of a 4-puttonyos Aszú, made for pure enjoyment and good conversation. The wine takes its name from the building that was once a smart gentlemen's club in the days when noblemen owned the great Tokaji estates.

ÉDES ÉLET 2003 A superb example of the late-harvest style made from top-quality aszú berries with the same level of residual sugar as a 6-puttonyos. An invigorating and joyful wine.

TOKAJI ASZÚ 6-PUTTONYOS 2000 Great structure and concentration with a strong personality. Árvay harmonises many different flavours in this complex wine.

TOKAJI ASZÚ 6-PUTTONYOS 1999 HÁRSLEVELŰ A memorable wine made from ripe Hárslevelű grapes, with the touch of a master winemaker.

ISTENHEGY VINEYARD

On well-drained south-southwest-facing slopes close to Rátka, this sunny vineyard benefits from the cool air that sweeps along the corridor of conical-shaped volcanic hills. It produces bone-dry Furmint with a positively mineral character and is quite an intense wine, best served with fresh river fish of the region. The colour and style of this accomplished wine is most unusual, and is the product of the skill and imagination of one of Tokaji's most gifted winemakers working in his native village, with grapes close to his heart.

HÉTSZŐLŐ

HÉTSZŐLŐ HAS BEEN one of the great estates of Tokaj since the Garay Family came from southern Hungary in 1502, purchasing seven vineyard plots on Tokaj Hill that they amalgamated into one estate, hence the name Hétszőlő ('seven vineyards').

FOLLOWING THE GARAYS, several Transylvanian princes owned the estate before it was taken over by the Austrian Treasury and then nationalised in 1948.

IN 1991 it was purchased by Grand Millesimes de France (GMF), the owners of Chateau Beychevelle in the Medoc. The Japanese distillery Suntory has a significant interest.

Hétszőlő

3910 Tokaj, Bajcsy-Zsilinszky utca 19-21
T: +36 47 352 009, F: +36 47 352 141
hetszolo@axelero.hu
www.tokaj.com
Directions: To Vineyard, go 2km from Tokaj on Road 38. The vineyard's name is clearly marked on one of the retaining walls. Cellars are located at Kossuth tér in Tokaj town centre.
Owner: GMF (France), Suntory (Japan)
Estate: 50ha under vine planted a density of 5,500 vines per hectare on a medium cordon.
Varieties planted: Furmint 70%, Hárslevelű 20%, Yellow Muscat and Kövérszőlő 10%
Tour and tasting cost: Ft 2,500
Visiting hours: 10:00-17:00
Languages spoken: French, English

FROM THE VERY OUTSET the new owners determined to make viticultural excellence their top priority. They replanted the whole vineyard with Furmint, Hárslevelű, Yellow Muscat, and Kövérszőlő.

ONE OF THE WORLD'S best-looking and best-maintained vineyards, Hétszőlő is superbly sited on the south-facing slopes of Tokaj Hill, where the dacite bedrock is overlain with a thick layer of loess. The vineyards are cared for by a team of employees, each entrusted with one hectare to work to the agreed standard and timetable but within their own timeframe, co-opting family participation if they so wish.

GMF APPOINTED DR. TIBOR KOVÁCS, one of Hungary's leading oenologists, as manager of the estate. A graduate of Kecskemét Horticultural College, Kovács prepared his doctoral thesis at the University of Montpellier in France, and has the additional advantage of speaking fluent French.

HÉTSZŐLŐ'S first 6-puttonyos Aszú, produced by Dr. Kovács and winemaker András Kanczler in 1995, revealed the breeding and class of this great vineyard. Hétszőlő has continued to produce outstanding wines ever since, including superb Aszú wines from both Hárslevelű and Kövérszőlő.

THE HÉTSZŐLŐ STYLE IS RICHLY HONEYED, elegant, and fruity. Some critics find the influence of the loess soil too pervasive, but whatever your personal taste preference we recommend that you include a sampling of these beautifully made wines in your itinerary. Hétszőlő's famous Rákóczi Cellars are near the winery in Kossuth Square, the centre of Tokaj. (In the region there are several 'Rákóczi Cellars', so for this site be careful to refer to the full winery name and town, Hétszőlő in Tokaj.)

THIS CELLAR has an important historical connection. Following the death of King Louis II at the battle of Mohács in 1526, besieged Hungarian nobles gathered in these cellars – here János Szapolyai, the most powerful northern landowner, was elected King of Hungary. As a result of his claims to the kingdom, Transylvania eventually became an independent princedom paying respect to Vienna and protection money to Istanbul for around 170 years.

HÉTSZŐLŐ IS DEVELOPING its organic viticulture and aims to become fully biodynamic over the next decade. Dr. Kovács is researching older clones of Furmint, planning to develop them to produce smaller grapes that he believes will give greater fruit concentration and flavour to his dry wines.

Range of Wines

DRY FURMINT 2005
Clean, fresh and fruity.
LATE-HARVEST HÁRS-LEVELŰ 2005 Pale in colour, soft honey bouquet, and ripe healthy fruit on the palate.
DESSEWFFY DRY SZAMORODNI 1998
A very polished wine with rich aromas and wonderfully dry finish.
ASZÚ 5-PUTTONYOS 2001 HÁRSLEVELŰ An absolutely delicious, superbly balanced wine with a long, smooth finish. Shows Hétszőlő and Hárslevelű at their best.
ASZÚ 6-PUTTONYOS 2000 Full, rich flavour with great complexity. A big, well-balanced wine that should progress well for many years yet.

HÉTSZŐLŐ VINEYARD

The 50-hectare estate is perfectly sited for the botrytisation of its grapes, as it spreads across the southern slopes of Tokaj Hill above the confluence of the Tisza and Bodrog.

Hétszőlő is beautifully maintained, continuing the old practice of appointing workers to carry out all the viticultural tasks in their allotted hectare of vineyard.

The hillside here is rather steeper than at Szarvas, and the new owners have had to build strong retaining walls to hold the loosely structured loess soils in wet conditions; the Hétszőlő name is emblazoned on one of them. Concrete tracks have been laid to carry off excess rainwater and allowing vineyard vehicles easier access to higher slopes in bad weather.

Furmint is planted on the middle and higher slopes, while Hárslevelű thrives around the skirt. The loess soil gives rich, honeyed wines that are softer and less masculine than those from clay soils, but fine nonetheless. The 2001 Aszú 5-puttonyos, for example, was a magnificent wine made in this vineyard during what was generally described as a difficult year.

ZOLTÁN DEMETER

ZOLTÁN DEMETER is the chief winemaker at Királyudvar, one of the largest Tokaji estates that we will visit in Tarcal. However, it is the custom that estate winemakers

Zoltán Demeter

3910 Tokaj, Vasvári Pál utca 3
T: +36 20 937 7074
demeterzoltan@demeterzoltan.hu
www.demeterzoltan.hu
Directions: From Kossuth tér walk along Gábor Bethlen utca, turn down József Attila utca and take the first left turn into Vasvári Pál utca.
Owner: Zoltán Demeter
Estate: 4.5ha in five different plots
Varieties planted: Furmint, Hárslevelű and Yellow Muscat
Visiting hours: By appointment
Languages spoken: English

are allowed to maintain their own family plots and make their own wines.

IT IS AN ENLIGHTENED APPROACH, allowing winemakers to explore ideas in their own vineyards or wineries before developing them for their employer. Thus Demeter is encouraged to give his imagination free reign when harvesting his 4.5 hectares, and he responds by producing superb late-harvest wines under his own label that are stocked by Monarchia Wines and the Terroir Club in Budapest, and by Monarchia MATT International in the USA.

AFTER GRADUATING from horticultural college, Demeter gained experience in Burgundy and California before joining Hétszőlő under Dr. Kovács. In 1996 he was appointed chief winemaker at Dégenfeld, and in 1999 moved on to Királyudvar where he worked with István Szepsy. He has since flowered in his own right as chief winemaker at Királyudvar, making extremely classy wines for Anthony Hwang.

DEMETER'S own plots are all in First Growth vineyards, the key to making great wines. Because there are limits to the quantity of wines that he can make privately, he focuses on quality and the style of wine that he most enjoys crafting.

A THOUGHTFUL AND PHILOSOPHICAL MAN with a deep passion for music, Demeter remarked during our interview that the most important lesson he had learnt from the master winemakers with whom he had worked was "how not to interfere with nature" when it comes to winemaking.

HE LIKES to be among his vines as often as possible because he finds them inspirational, and they generously transmit their energy to him – a claim that any keen gardener will understand. In the winery he eschews commercial yeasts, enzymes, and chemical treatments, and all his wines have purity of taste.

Range of Wines

DRY FURMINT 2003 Concentrated flavours, elegant and silky smooth. Demeter produces three single-vineyard dry Furmint wines from loess, clay, and nyirok soils in the Szerelmi, Veres, and Lapis vineyards. They are all exquisite wines with subtle differences and are exclusively available through the Terroir Club in Budapest.

LATE-HARVEST 2003 Pale green with rich floral aromas and 120g/l sugar that you hardly notice as it is so well-balanced. A superb example of its type exclusively available through Monarchia Wines.

ASZÚ 6-PUTTONYOS 2002 Another wonderfully balanced wine. Great concentration of fruit with lively acids to offset the natural sweetness. A subtle wine made with great sensitivity.

DEMETER IS ONE OF THE MOST GIFTED WINE-MAKERS IN TOKAJ, helping raise the profile of the region's wines. He is the kind of vintner who does not rest on his laurels but continues to develop even more stylish and exciting wines. If you are ever offered a glass of one of his wines to taste, simply say 'yes please'.

DOBOGÓ

THE DOBOGÓ WINERY, in the very heart of Tokaj, takes its name from the clippity-clop of horses' hooves on the cobblestones of the streets as they brought the harvest into the winery. Owned by Izabella Zwack, the dynamic young wine merchant in Budapest, the winery is run by talented winemaker Attila Domokos.

DOMOKOS' WINES have already won a heap of medals, which is hardly surprising given the company's uncompromising approach to producing top-quality grapes

from controlled yields in First Growth vineyards around Tokaj Hill and Mád.

DOBOGÓ NOT ONLY MAKES FINE WINES WELL, but markets them imaginatively. The late-harvest wine Mylitta is stylishly labelled, telling the story of Izabella's Great Aunt Mylitta, who was the muse of Endre Ady, one Hungary's greatest poets.

Dobogó
3910 Tokaj, Dózsa György utca 1
T: +36 47 552 147
F: +36 47 552 148
dobogotokaj@t-online.hu
www.dobogo.hu
Directions: Dózsa György utca runs off Bem utca north of Kossuth tér.
Owner: Izabella Zwack
Estate: 8ha in the Mád Basin and on Tokaj Hill
Varieties planted: Furmint, Hárslevelű, Yellow Muscat
Tour and tasting cost: Ft 2,500
Visiting hours: 10:00-16:00 by appointment
Languages spoken: English, Italian

IN SUMMER the winery terrace makes an agreeable place to taste the Dobogó wines, which often include sampling their specially made Tyrolean blue cheese matured with aszú grapes – a perfect accompaniment to the award-winning 2000 Aszú 6-puttonyos.

THE LIVELY DOBOGÓ TEAM likes to keep busy with different projects. They are producing a red wine from Kékfrankos – not eligible for Tokaji appellation – and are working on the concept of a sparkling rosé made from Pinot Noir grapes grown in Tokaj. These are interesting diversions, but they do not distract Domokos from his main objective of continually developing the Dobogó range of Tokaji wines for the domestic market and export to the USA, UK, Sweden, Holland, Poland, Russia, and other nations.

VISITORS CAN ALSO PURCHASE DOBOGÓ'S own wine vinegar, matured in cask for 11 months.

Range of Wines

DRY FURMINT 2005 Light golden colour with generous fruit and a flinty nose. The palate unfolds to present a full-bodied wine with a creamy finish that we expect to hold up well in the glass for a few years yet. Izabella recommends it with a tuna and avocado salad. This is the wine that prompted British wine authority Stephen Spurrier to ask: Is Furmint the new Gruner Veltliner?

MYLITTA 2005 Pale yellow colour but a full-bodied wine with lovely white-peach flavours. A charming aperitif that also goes well with fresh cheeses or ripe white peaches.

ASZÚ 6-PUTTONYOS 2000 Deep golden colour with a trace of orange at the rim. A wonderful bouquet of dried fruits and honey delight the nose. On the palate there is the taste of ripe fruit balanced with firm acids and a long finish.

Hímesudvar
3910 Tokaj, Bem út 2
T: +36 47 352 416
tokaji@himesudvar.hu
www.himesudvar.hu
Directions: Bem út runs north from Kossuth tér. Look for a gate in the wall for the entry to the Hímesudvar Winery and garden.

HÍMESUDVAR

FROM THE VERY ESTABLISHMENT OF HIS COMPANY, Péter Várhelyi determined to take a purist approach to his winemaking. He supplements the produce of his own three-hectare vineyard with top-quality grapes from trusted local growers to produce a limited range of top-class wines.

HIS VINEYARD WORK IS IMPRESSIVE. He uses short-spur training to encourage strong and vigorous shoots, which he trains carefully to ensure maximum ripeness of fruit. His winemaking is careful and deliberate in his search for perfection: he uses new gönci barrels for cask fermentation and ageing in order to give his wines extra body and character. Hímesudvar produces around 20,000 bottles a year, most of which is sold to local restaurants and cellar visitors.

HIS WINERY HAS BEEN converted from the old hunting lodge of 16th-century Hungarian king János Szapolyai. The entrance to the cellar is through a walled gate, serving as a reminder that the property was originally a classic motte with earthen walls (hence its name), built after the Magyar Conquest of 896. The garden terrace is a pleasant and peaceful place to taste, or to simply enjoy a glass of fine wine. The small and friendly winery shop lists their award-winning dry Furmint, Cuvee, and Aszú at very competitive prices.

ERZSÉBET

ERZSÉBET, owned since 1994 by the Pracser Family, cultivates 13 hectares of vineyard in First Growths around Tarcal and Mád. Their cellar dates from the early 1700s, and from 1733-98 was used to store the Aszú wines purchased by Czarina Elizabeth at the Russian Imperial Court – Cossack troops were sent to accompany the valuable shipments back to St. Petersburg. The barrels of wines were carted

overland to the Baltic port of Danzig, from where they continued their journey across the sea to the capital.

Erzsébet
3910 Tokaj, Bem utca 16
T: +36 47 353 547, +36 20 9259 931 (mobile for English)
info@erzsebetpince.hu
www.erzsebetpince.hu
Directions: Bem utca leads from Kossuth tér and curls around the top of town.

AS WINES WERE NOT GENERALLY sold in bottle until the 1850s, Gönci barrels, coopered from Zemplén oak, were made to fit the carts. The 136-litre size was considered ideal for handling on the long journey.

BOTH MIKLÓS AND ERZSÉBET PRACSER trained as horticultural engineers, and their wines are made to a high standard from selected plots in First Growths. Their full-bodied dry Furmint is harvested from a plot next to that of István Szepsy in Király; while the semisweet

Hárslevelű from the Zafír vineyard in Tarcal has rich honey and apricot flavours. The 5-puttonyos Aszú 1999 was made from wonderfully ripe grapes and is showing well with lovely apricot flavours. The 5-puttonyos Aszú 1993 is in superb condition.

THE WINERY HAS BEEN MODERNISED with brand-new visitor facilities, including two well-furnished rooms and an apartment to let at reasonable rates. This delightful panzió and winery is run by the charming Erzsébet Pracser, whose daughter is fluent in English.

BOTT WINERY

THIS RELATIVELY NEW START-UP WINERY, located in the old cellar row tucked underneath Tokaj Hill's famous Szerelmi Vineyard, recently announced itself with some beautiful wines.

JUDIT BOTT, now married to József Bodó, made her name at Füleky before setting up her own business with her husband.

HER 2006 DRY FURMINT showed exotic flavours on a rich mineral base, and the sweetness of the 2006 Bott-rytis – a memorably named late-harvest wine with 120g/l residual sugar – was held in check by vibrant acids. The 2006 Aszú is a remarkable wine already. It is superbly balanced and has the same depth and complexity of the more-established Aszú wines. Bott is distributed through the Terroir Club in Budapest. Visitors are welcome by appointment, and Judit speaks excellent English.

> **Bott Winery**
> 3910 Tokaj, Szerelmi Cellar Row
> T: +36 20 240 3855 (mobile)
> judit.bodo@bottpince.hu
> www.bottpince.hu
> **Directions:** The cellar row is right opposite the Tokaj train station.

TARCAL

TO THE WEST OF TOKAJ HILL, the historical village of Tarcal is home to many significant attractions and notable buildings – as well as some of Tokaji's most outstanding wineries and vineyards.

ACCOMMODATIONS IN TARCAL

GRÓF DÉGENFELD CASTLE HOTEL

The Gróf Dégenfeld Castle Hotel stands in beautiful parkland, once part of a royal estate, in front of the Dégenfeld Winery on the northern outskirts of Tarcal, seven kilometres from Tokaj.

The four-star luxury hotel exudes Old-World charm, but its 20 double bedrooms are air-conditioned and have satellite and Internet connections. The beautiful library and elegant salon evoke a 19th-century atmosphere, making it one of the finest and most comfortable hotels in the region.

There is a good-sized outdoor swimming pool and a tennis court, and sauna and massage treatments are available. Horseback riding and boat trips on the Bodrog can be arranged for visitors.

Hotel room rates and booking procedures are set out on the informative Website.

Gróf Dégenfeld Castle Hotel
3915 Tarcal, Terézia kert 9
T: +36 47 580 400
hotel@degenfeld.hu
www.hotelgrofdegenfeld.com

ANDRÁSSY HOTEL

This new luxury 42-bedroom vino-therapeutic hotel in the centre of Tarcal is due to open in December 2007, and will offer guests a wide range of health-spa treatments based on the latest scientific discoveries about ageing.

The hotel features a unique cellar spa with saunas, massage, indoor swimming pools, Jacuzzis, and fitness equipment. The accommodation is spacious and sumptuous and there will be a first-class restaurant offering the award-winning Andrássy wines to visitors.

The Andrássy Website gives full details of the hotel and spa, accommodation options and reservation procedures. Room rates include breakfast and use of the wellness facilities. Visits to the winery can be arranged through the hotel.

Andrássy Hotel
3915 Tarcal, Fő utca 94
T: +36 47 380 220
F: +36 47 580 026
sales@andrassy.hu
www.andrassy.hu

DINING IN TARCAL

GRÓF DÉGENFELD CASTLE HOTEL RESTAURANT

The hotel restaurant (see accommodations for directions) has a well-chosen menu to complement the Dégenfeld wines, as well as those of other producers. Many of the wines are offered by the glass. The main dining room

is extremely elegant and superbly furnished, but it is more fun to dine alfresco on the terrace in front of the hotel. The menu features some innovative touches to show off the Dégenfeld wines.

Gróf Dégenfeld Castle Hotel Restaurant
3915 Tarcal, Terézia kert
T: +36 47 580 400

ANDRÁSSY HOTEL RESTAURANT PASSIONE

Opening in December 2007 along with its host hotel, the new Passione restaurant has been designed to offer a relaxed and relaxing atmosphere. The menu will offer international cuisine, regional specialities, and a wide selection of wines by the glass.

**Andrássy Hotel
Restaurant Passione**
3915 Tarcal, Fő utca 94
T: +36 47 380 220
F: +36 47 580 026
sales@andrassy.hu
www.andrassy.hu

Guests will find an outdoor area for alfresco dining in summer months, and a bar cellar for those who like to take a cool drink out of the sun.

KOVÁCS KÁLMÁN

Coming through Tarcal from Tokaj, look for the right turn to Bodrogkeresztúr to find just the place for tasting typical Hungarian fare with wines made in the traditional oxidative style. This is an enjoyable destination, particularly if you have a Hungarian-speaking friend with you to explain a little about the cuisine and wines.

Kovács Kálmán
3915 Tarcal,
Bodrogkeresztúri utca
47-49
T: +36 47 380 849,
+36 47 380 444
F: +36 47 380 255

Don't be too surprised if you find yourself dining alongside another Kovács – none other than Kokó, the former WBA world featherweight champion turned TV presenter, who owns several hectares of vineyards on Tokaj Hill. Kálmán Kovács maintains them, and the celebrity pugilist makes frequent visits to the region to find out how his vines are progressing.

WINERIES

GRÓF DÉGENFELD

WHEN THE TOKAJ VITICULTURAL ASSOCIATION was formed in 1857 to address the problem of replacing lost markets after political changes in northern Europe, Count Imre Dégenfeld and his fellow cofounders recommended that they focus all their attention on improving the quality of their grapes. Their goal was to make wines so good that the world could not ignore them.

NOW 150 YEARS LATER, the Dégenfeld Family still believes that top-quality fruit is the most important determinant of the quality of their wines. When they developed their new 100-hectare estate in 1994, they based it on First

Gróf Dégenfeld

3915 Tarcal, Terézia kert 9
T: +36 47 380 173
F: +36 47 380 149
degenfeld@degenfeld.hu
www.degenfeld.hu
Directions: From Tokaj take
Road 38 north to the northern
outskirts of Tarcal. From
Disznókő Winery take Road 38
south for 5km. The winery is
behind the Dégenfeld Castle
Hotel.
Owner: Gróf Dégenfeld Family
Estate: 100ha, 80ha under
vine planted at a density of
6,800 vines per hectare on a
low cordon.
Varieties planted: Furmint
70%, Hárslevelű 25%, Yellow
Muscat 5%
Tour and tasting cost: Ft 2,500
Visiting hours: 10:00-17:00
Restaurant hours:
12:00-22:00
Languages spoken: English,
German

Growth vineyards around Tarcal and Mád in both clay and loess soils. The Dégenfelds are the proud owners of 12 hectares in the nearby Mézes Mály Great Growth, 25 hectares in Galambos, and a good plot in Terézia on the hill above the winery.

TO PROCESS THEIR PRECIOUS grapes the family asked Ferenc Salamin to design a modern winery using local materials wherever possible. The result is a stylish, clean-cut, contemporary working winery constructed with local stone and wonderful overarching oak beams. Good natural light pours into the building, which has been erected over the fine old cellars dug deep into the tuff of Terézia Hill.

SINCE ITS RE-CREATION DÉGENFELD has recruited a stream of brilliant young winemakers. Zoltán Demeter and Sarolta Bárdos were followed by Gábor Rakaczki, who has been at the helm for the last seven years. Their work has resulted in a hatful of international awards for their outstanding wines.

AT THE 2006 PANNON BORMUSTRA (Pannon Wine Festival), Hungary's most prestigious wine competition attended by all top winemakers, the Gróf Dégenfeld Aszú 6-puttonyos was voted wine of the year, with the internation-

al panel of judges citing its rich aroma, intensity of flavour and high mineral extract. Andante, another award-winning wine, may mean 'moderately slow' in musical terms, but this late-harvest Furmint that Rakaczki produced in 2005 set the judges' pulses racing.

DÉGENFELD HAS perfected an elegant and charming style that is reflected in its complete range of wines. It was one of the first wineries to reveal the delights of Muscat Lunel as a varietal wine, and now offers semisweet and late-harvest Hárslevelű. Wines may be purchased from the hotel, or in the Dégenfeld shop in Kossuth tér in Tokaj.

THIS IS AN ATTRACTIVE estate that was voted runner-up to Winery of the Year in 2006, and should you decide to visit, allow time afterwards to walk or drive up to the St. Terézia chapel atop the hill behind the winery to look out over the vast Great Hungarian Plain.

Range of Wines

DRY FURMINT 2005 Pale straw-yellow in colour, fruity and fresh.

MUSCATEL LUNEL 2005 SEMIDRY The bouquet is positively Muscat. Its brisk acids and fresh fruit make it a pleasant light wine.

HÁRSLEVELŰ 2002 LATE-HARVEST SEMISWEET With a pale green tint, and a lovely honey and linden-flower bouquet. Firm body with playful acids.

ASZÚ 5-PUTTONYOS 1999 Intensive bouquet. Sound structure. Honey and apricot on the palate and a nice long finish.

ASZÚ 6-PUTTONYOS 2000 A wonderfully understated and elegant wine. Less intensive but still charming. Well-balanced with good concentration.

ANDANTE LATE-HARVEST FURMINT 2003 A delicious wine that has been made with very ripe grapes, with the class to be enjoyed now but the character to age a little more.

GALAMBOS VINEYARD

The Galambos Vineyard is located above the Sós Borház Panzió alongside Road 38 to Mád. Most of its well-drained 40 hectares are owned by Dégenfeld, and they enjoy south-southwest exposure 130-160 metres above sea level, in prime position to benefit from the low-lying mists of the region.

The rhyolite rock base is covered with a brown forest-clay soil rich in humus. This earth is typical of the foothills and has good structure and water retention. It has a neutral pH and a well-balanced mineral content that yields firm wines with what locals call 'fire' in them. They are blended with the more-honeyed and softer wines produced in the loess soils of Tokaj Hill.

Királyudvar
3915 Tarcal, Fő utca 92
T: +36 47 380 111
F: +36 47 380 952
kiralyudvar@hu.inter.net
www.kiralyudvar.com
Directions: From Tokaj take Road 38 to Tarcal town centre. The entrance to Királyudvar is just past the Andrássy Hotel.
Owner: Hwang Family
Estate: 109ha, 80ha under vine planted at a density of 6,000 vines per hectare on a low cordon.
Varieties planted:
Furmint 64%, Hárslevelű 32%, Yellow Muscat 4%
Visiting hours:
Professional visits by appointment only. Királyudvar hosts open house days several times a year.

KIRÁLYUDVAR

OF ALL THE NEW TOKAJI ESTATES, the origin of Királyudvar, formed in 1997, is the most intriguing. It began with a family birthday party in Budapest where successful Chinese-American businessman Anthony Hwang first tasted István Szepsy's 1993 Aszú 6-Puttonyos. He was so impressed with the wine, the vintner, and what he was trying to accomplish that he decided to invest in Tokaj, asking Szepsy to help him.

KIRÁLYUDVAR acquired prime sites in First Growth vineyards around Tarcal, Mád and Bodrogkeresztúr, and appointed Zoltán Demeter as winemaker. Working with Szepsy, Demeter produced a series of brilliant, innovative wines starting with the 1999 Aszú 6-Puttonyos, the exceptional 1999 Aszú 6-Puttonyos Lapis, and Cuvee Ilona, a sophisticated late-harvest wine made to exacting stan-

dards. The 2002 Aszú 6-Puttonyos was voted Champion Wine at the prestigious 2007 Pannon Bormustra.

THE FOLLOWING year the winery produced an outstanding single-vineyard Dry Furmint from Úrágya, and has since gone on to develop some new and very fine dry and semidry wines.

IN 2006 HWANG AND SZEPSY reached an amicable agreement to go their own ways – Szepsy to devote more time to developing his own 62-hectare estate with his family; Hwang and Demeter to further explore new wine concepts and build the Királyudvar brand worldwide. Already distributed in the USA, Canada, and the UK, Királyudvar has been successfully launched in China in good time for the 2008 Olympic Games.

HWANG IS EXCITED BY THE NEW CHALLENGE. A genuine enthusiast who first came to appreciate fine wine during his student years at Cambridge University, he is also owner of the celebrated Domaine Huet in France's Loire Valley. Determined to offer refined, elegant, pure and precise wines, Hwang says he wants "the stones to speak for themselves."

HWANG IS ALSO COMMITTED to biodynamic viticulture because "it makes good business sense." He believes he will get better-quality fruit earlier and reduce the risk of bad weather spoiling his crops.

Range of Wines

DRY FURMINT 2006 Pure and precise with 12.8 degrees of alcohol and beautifully balanced.

SEMIDRY 2006 This style is difficult to make, but Demeter has done wonders with it – not that he is yet satisfied. Cultured and attractive, this is a style to grace the finest cuisine.

CUVEE PATRICIA This late-harvest wine, made from mixed bunches of botrytised and non-botrytised grapes, has the distinct house style, exquisitely light and refreshing.

CUVEE ILONA 2003 A top-quality Cuvee wine made in great vintages to a very high standard. Its concentration of fruit and superb balance makes it a fitting wine for special occasions.

ASZÚ 6-PUTTONYOS 2002 A pale golden colour with wonderful fresh fruit aromas and a strong mineral backbone and yet on the palate it is creamy and as soft as satin. Voted Champion Wine at Pannon Bormustra 2007.

ASZÚ 6-PUTTONYOS LAPIS 1999 Pale in colour with a rich, honeyed nose, the sugar is underpinned by fine acids – an extraordinary wine that is complimentary to both vineyard and winemakers.

LAPIS VINEYARD

Lapis is a huge 100-hectare vineyard mostly with a southeasterly aspect. It is divided into several parts, the most interesting of which is the section known as the Greater Lapis on the middle and upper reaches of the slope.

The Greater Lapis's 30 or so hectares produce wines of wonderful character. The 1999 Királyudvar Aszú 6-Puttonyos Lapis harvested from here is a superbly structured wine of extraordinary finesse and breathtaking elegance, despite its straw-pale colour. The 2002 was unanimously voted Champion Wine by all seven of the international judges at the 2007 Pannon Bormustra.

What makes the difference is that the well-drained soils in the middle and top section are clay mixed with broken rock, yielding strong yet very fine wines of singular character. If there was ever to be a reclassification of Tokaji vineyards, we would expect Greater Lapis to be a contender for Great Growth status.

IN 2006 KIRÁLYUDVAR released a dry Furmint and a demi-sec wine that reflected this approach. In both cases the grapes were picked at the precise moment of ripeness, pressed very gently, and fermented to the optimum degree by careful temperature control. Given gentle oak treatment they have retained all the flavour of the grape, and yet have body and presence.

THOUGH THE ESTATE is largely planted with old Furmint vines, Hwang also recognises the potential of Hárslevelű and Yellow Muscat to make very fine wines, and is developing mono-sepage vineyards while taking care to select rootstock to match the soil conditions of each site.

AS ONE WOULD EXPECT of a successful international businessman, Hwang is decisive about the future of Tokaj. He believes its dry and semi-sweet wines have a great future, and is deeply impressed with the Tokaji terroirs that produce such outstanding Aszú wines. And Hwang is completely in communion with those other top Tokaji winemakers in the conviction that the best way to make Tokaj better-known is to produce truly great wines.

ANDRÁSSY

ANDRÁSSY IS A RELATIVELY new winery founded in 1999 by József Szabó, whose successful Naturland health-care business allowed him to invest in the Tokaj region that he loves.

Andrássy
3915 Tarcal, Fő utca 94
T: +36 47 380 220
F: +36 47 580 026
info@andrassy.hu
www.andrassy.hu
Directions: From Tokaj take Road 38 to the centre of Tarcal. The winery is behind the Andrássy Hotel.
Owner: József Szabó
Estate: 20ha under vine in Szentkereszt planted at a density of 5,500 vines per hectare on a low cordon.
Varieties planted: Furmint, Hárslevelű, Yellow Muscat
Tour and tasting cost: From Ft 2,500
Visiting hours: 9:00-16:00
Languages spoken: English

THE WINERY, adjacent to the luxurious new 42-bedroom vino-therapeutic hotel described earlier, is built over the cellars of the Rákóczi Mansion in Tarcal.

MOST OF THE 20 HECTARES are in the First Growth Szentkereszt Vineyard at Bodrogkeresztúr. Its loess soils help define the charac-

ter of the Andrássy wines, made by experienced vintner László Gervald. Gervald has a wonderful touch with all three of the main varieties planted – Furmint, Hárslevelű and Yellow Muscat. He also knows how to combine them in classy Aszú wines that have picked up a heap of gold medals in international competitions.

THE MARKETING OF ANDRÁSSY WINES is adeptly handled, with distribution at home and abroad directed at smaller specialist importers with strong links to the hotel and restaurant trade. Sales in the important Far-Eastern markets have been boosted by the award of a Gold Medal for the 2000 Aszú 6-Puttonyos at the Shanghai International Wine Challenge.

THESE ARE EXCITING TIMES AT ANDRÁSSY. The 2006 vintage is expected to produce more superb wines – watch out for the Yellow Muscat Aszú-Eszencia when it is released.

THE ANDRÁSSY NAME was made famous by Count Gyula Andrássy, appointed the first Hungarian prime minister following the Compromise of 1867 with Austria. With Gervald at the helm, the new winery is poised to make the name well-known again.

Range of Wines

DRY FURMINT 2005 An elegant and graceful wine showing the advantage of ripe fruit and fine acids. Saltwater fish will show it off well.

HÁRSLEVELŰ 2005 The honeyed, flowery, fruity fragrance is attractive to the nose, and these flavours are extended to the palate in a very classy wine. Be bold and try it with some creamy blue cheese.

MUSCAT LUNEL 2005 The grapes are bought in from a sunny site in the Teleki Vineyard, and the fruity aromas and semi-sweet flavours delight the palate. This is an aperitif wine but it is fun with lighter desserts.

ASZÚ 4-PUTTONYOS 1999 The debut wine beautifully made with honey-rich tones and a pleasant bittersweet finish.

ASZÚ 6-PUTTONYOS 2000 Ripe Furmint grapes and fine acids underpin this well-made, warm vintage wine.

MUSCAT LUNEL ASZÚ-ESZENCIA 2000 A remarkable wine made from well-botrytised Muscat grapes with honey-rich flavours developed by the loess soil. A world-class wine.

TOKAJICUM WINE ESTATE

LÁSZLÓ MAJOROS is one of three partners that have built a fine modern winery at the foot of the Perőcz Vineyard just south of Tarcal. The winery's 20 hectares are spread over eight growths around Tarcal and Mád,

Tokajicum Wine Estate
3915 Tarcal,
Tokajicum utca
T: +36 47 580 017
F: +36 47 580 018
info@tokajicum.hu
www.tojajicum.hu
Directions: Coming from Tokaj on Road 38 look for the new winery (up a short drive on the right) as you approach Tarcal.

and reflect Majoros's view that the clay soils of the Mád Basin are more forceful, yielding wines with higher acidity and alcohol, while the loess soils of Tarcal provide wines with greater aroma and elegance.

IN MANY WAYS, Majoros reminds us of the young István Szepsy. He is fiercely determined to focus all his efforts on making distinctive wines true to the nature of the First Growth vineyards which he loves. And he has the same eye for detail in every aspect of fieldwork and cellar-work.

IN THE VINEYARD he is aware of the importance of having the right clones and encouraging natural yeasts. He leaves his grapes on the vine until the optimal point when natural sugar, acids and aromas are well-balanced. In the cellar he is ever-watchful, seeking the best conditions to make and age his wines. He is currently experimenting with different types and sizes of oak barrel to find the one or ones that best suit his wines. He uses reductive technology to produce his base wines but limits the use of sulphur to the bottling process.

HIS INDUSTRY has been rewarded with a Decanter Award for his 1998 Aszú 6-Puttonyos. He is doubly proud because it was a difficult and small vintage. We were also impressed with his unfiltered dry Furmint (the first one we have come across in Tokaj), and his finely balanced late-harvest cuvée.

THIS YOUNG VINTNER, who consulted both Szepsy and János Árvay before setting up his winery, is worth following for his skills and dedication to his task.

DOROGI BROTHERS

ALTHOUGH the Dorogi Brothers jointly run the business, it was István the winemaker who produced the delightful 2003 Cuvee Anna, named after his newborn niece. The wine has the sweet aroma of honey and ripe pears.

DOROGI HARVESTS six hectares from vineyards around Tarcal, and make good-quality varietal wines as well as Aszú 6-puttonyos. The 2002 vintage shows nice concentration, with Hárslevelű evident on the nose and Furmint on the palate. With 220g/l sugar and 12g/l acidity, it is nicely balanced.

IN THEIR SEARCH FOR NEWER, fresher flavours, the brothers are experimenting with Furmint blended with Kövérszőlő.

The latter variety grows well around Tarcal, where the research station conducted a great deal of development work in the 1990s.

IT IS ENCOURAGING to see young winemakers experimenting with new varieties to back up their range, which includes dry Furmint, Hárslevelű, Yellow Muscat and Kövérszőlő.

Dorogi Brothers
3915 Tarcal, Arany János utca 7
T: +36 20 9576 640
dorogi@freemail.hu
Directions: From Tokaj take Road 38 through the centre of Tarcal and turn left into Arany János utca at Sport tér.

KIKELET

STEPHANIE BERECZ and her husband Zsolt currently own three hectares and rent another two hectares, making varietal wines, Szamorodnis and Aszús to an extremely high standard.

AT DISZNÓKŐ, Stephanie followed János Árvay as

Kikelet

3915 Tarcal, Könyves
Kálmán utca 62
T: +36 30 636 9046
bstephkik@hotmail.com
Directions: From Tokaj
take Road 38 north and
the first right past
Királyudvar Winery,
where the road forks.

Chief Winemaker, but has quickly made her mark as an independent vintner with wines of extraordinary delicacy and delightful fragrance. Her debut wines were sensational, and the winery's future looks very promising.

POSTA PINCE

FURTHER ALONG KÖNYVES KÁLMÁN UTCA, this small family cellar, run by Lajos Posta, makes wonderfully elegant, traditional-style Aszú wines. The finishing touches are provided by Lajos' daughter Ildikó, currently the winemaker at Disznókő.

Posta Pince

3915 Tarcal,
Könyves Kálmán utca 18
T: +36 47 380 444
Directions: From Tokaj take
Road 38 to Tarcal centre, and the
first right after Királyudvar Winery.

PÁLL

CALIFORNIA-TRAINED WINEMAKER ROLAND PÁLL is determined to use the family's 12 hectares of loess soils on Tokaj Hill (seven of which are in the Kinnai Vineyard) to produce a range of stylish, fruity wines. His first efforts have been well-received and we believe he will make even better wines. The winery also owns a small family-run panzio with comfortable attic bedrooms.

Páll

3915 Tarcal, Szondi utca 3/2
T: +36 47 380 016, +36 30 955 2167 (mobile)
F: +36 47 380 639
info@pallpince.hu
www.pallpince.hu
Directions: From Tokaj take Road 38 through
Tarcal. Turn right into Botond utca just before
the Dégenfeld Hotel, and then the first left.

KOVÁCS KÁLMÁN

THIS WINERY MAKES some very acceptable oxidative-style wines, such as the fresh and invigorating 1993 Aszú 5-puttonyos that we tasted. The winery also serves food in its cellar.

Kovács Kálmán

3915 Tarcal,
Bodrogkeresztúri utca 47-49
T: +36 47 380 849, +36 47 380 444
F: +36 47 380 255

BODROGKERESZTÚR AND BODROGKISFALUD

THESE TWO SMALL VILLAGES are both a few kilometres from Tokaj on Road 38, following the Bodrog River as it meanders peacefully towards Sárospatak. There are better accommodation and dining options in nearby Tokaj, Tarcal, Erdőbénye or Mád, all of which are within a 15-minute drive. It is possible to take a boat from Tokaj to Bodrogkeresztúr, and visit a winery before the return voyage. Contact Tourinform Tokaj for details.

WINERIES

DERESZLA

DERESZLA BELONGS to the d'Aulan Family, former proprietors of Champagne Piper-Heidsieck and now owners of Chateau Sansonnet Grand Cru St. Emilion, Chateau Valrose Alienor in St. Estephe, and the Alta Vista Winery in Mendoza, Argentina.

Dereszla
3916 Bodrogkeresztúr, Felső utca 2
T & F: +36 47 396 004
dereszla@dereszla.com
www.dereszla.com
Directions: From Tokaj follow Road 38 to Bodrogkeresztúr; from Disznókő continue along Road 37 for 8km before turning right at the signpost to Bodrogkeresztúr. The Dereszla Winery is prominently signed.
Owner: The d'Aulan Family (France), Edonia
Estate: 50ha, with 17.5ha under vine planted at a density of 5,500 vines per hectare on a low cordon
Varieties planted: Furmint 55%, Hárslevelű 40%, Yellow Muscat 5%
Tour and tasting cost: From Ft 2,500
Visiting hours: 10:00-17:00
Languages spoken: English, French

THE FAMILY STRIVES for excellence at all its fine-wine properties, and Patrick d'Aulan is committed to matching the standards set by István Szepsy, whom he sees as the lodestar for all Tokaji winemakers.

DERESZLA TAKES ITS NAME from the vineyard on the slopes above the winery, which offers delightful views of the Bodrog gently wending its way east through the region's water meadows and marshes. The winery has plots in seven locations around the village and on Tokaj Hill in loess and nyirok soils. Furmint and Hárslevelű play an important role in the varietal structure of the estate, which also gets some extraordinary results from its Muscat.

THE FIRST WINES were made in the 2000 vintage when Nicholas Godebski, the French oenologist with many years of experience working in Tokaj, produced some stunning debut wines. The Chief Winemaker today is László Kalocsai, who has been actively involved with the Tarcal Research Centre in developing Kabar, the Bouvier cross with Hárslevelű variety authorised for use in Tokaj appellation wines from January 2007.

KALOCSAI ALSO OVERSAW the development of the modern winery and bottling hall across the road, a necessary complement to the 16th-century cellars of the original winery. A brand-new visitor reception area has been added where the range of Chateau Dereszla wines can be tasted, including the 2000 Aszú 6-puttonyos that won a top Decanter Award and a rating of 96 points from *Wine Spectator*. Patrick d'Aulan and his team are well on track to reach the standards set by their lodestar.

Range of Wines

CHATEAU DERESZLA T 10 2005 The code-name given to the Bouvier/Hárslevelű cross now called Kabar, an early-ripening variety, authorised from January 2007. It was developed at Dereszla as an insurance policy against poor autumn weather. Fermented in new oak, we noted pronounced Hárslevelű aromas and flavours, and will watch the performance of this new variety with interest.

DRY FURMINT ZSADÁNY 2003 Single-vineyard wine underpinned by mineral strength and fine acids. Bone dry, yet very fruity.

LATE-HARVEST MUSCAT RESERVE 2003 A classy Muscat that sees little wood and is fresher and more invigorating for it. 260g/l sugar and 10.4 acidity.

ASZÚ 5-PUTTONYOS 2000 We liked everything about this wine. The bouquet is rich and the fruity palate stirred by invigorating acidity. Good length.

ASZÚ 6-PUTTONYOS 2000 Greater concentration than the 5-puttonyos with a spiciness that both intrigues and delights. The wine is developing slowly and is expected to last a long time.

ASZÚ-ESZENCIA 2000 A single-vineyard wine from Henye Hill with a rich aroma and taste that lives up to its 'essence' description. Henye is an open-hill vineyard lying between the revered Mézes Mály and Dereszla vineyards.

CHATEAU DERESZLA SZAMORODNI EXPERIENCE 2003 An extremely well-made dry Szamorodni from Furmint grapes with a sherry-like nose and firm, bold acidity.

FÜLEKY

FÜLEKY OPENED ITS CELLAR DOORS in 1998 on the initiative of Countess Isabella Walderdorff and other South Tyrolean Partners, but negotiations for its sale to Hungarian wine enthusiast Péter Lovas have recently been concluded.

LOVAS HAS DETERMINED to modernise the winery and refurbish the 18th-century manor house to include visitor reception facilities and accommodation. We understand that there are also plans to increase the current vineyard holding to 25 hectares in the different soils of Mád, Tarcal and Szegi.

> **Füleky**
> 3916 Bodrogkeresztúr,
> Iskola köz 15
> T & F: +36 47 396 478
> fuleky@fuleky-tokaj.com
> **Directions:** Iskola köz
> runs up from the main
> Road 38 from the centre
> of the village.

FÜLEKY'S FIRST WINEMAKER was the talented Judit Bott, who has started her own company in Tokaj. She has been succeeded by György Brezovcik, who honed his winemaking skills at Dereszla. Brezovcik plans to continue to produce the refined and elegant wines, such as the late-harvest Pallas, for which Füleky has become known. Pale in colour, it is a clean, crisp wine with generous pear and peach flavours. The 2005 dry Furmint is well balanced with marked fruit concentration.

TOKAJ NOBILIS

THIS SMALL SIX-HECTARE ESTATE is owned by the husband-and-wife team of Sarolta Bárdos and Péter Molnár, who are notable chief winemakers at Béres and Patricius respectively.

WE HAVE PREVIOUSLY MENTIONED the custom in Tokaji that allows estate winemakers to run their own small family estates. In this case the young couple acquired two carefully chosen hillside sites in the Barakonyi and Csirke-mál vineyards near Bodrogkisfalud.

Tokaj Nobilis

3916 Bodrogkeresztúr, Kossuth út 103
T & F: +36 47 396 424
Mobile: +36 20 391 8328
bardos@tokajnobilis.hu
www.tokajnobilis.hu
Directions: Take Road 38 from
Tokaj and as you approach
Bodrogkeresztúr look for the first
pedestrian crossing. Tokaj Nobilis is
on the left in a long, low, white-paint-
ed farmhouse with an old wine
press in the front garden.
Tour and tasting cost:
From Ft 2,500

AS ONE WOULD EXPECT from two accomplished winemakers, they set out to
make top-quality, handcrafted wines
that express the unique qualities of their
terroirs. We tasted barrel samples of
three varietal wines from the 2006 vintage, and two of the house specialities.

THE DRY FURMINT aroused our interest, as both husband and wife have produced award-winning wines for their
employers. The Nobilis wines, from different terroirs, make their own mark.
The Furmint, fermented in oak and left
on its lees for a month or so, has plen-
ty of flavour and is well-supported by its
fine acids.

WE ALSO ADMIRED the graceful and
elegant late-harvest Kövérszőlő with 70
g/l of residual sugar: harvest conditions
were not perfect for the more tempera-
mental Yellow Muscat that needs to be picked when sugar-must levels are
around 178 g/l.

THE MAIN SPECIALITIES of the house are the late-
harvest Amicus blend of Furmint (90%) and
Kövérszőlő (10%), and the Aszú 6-puttonyos.
Both are fermented in oak. The 2006 vintage
Amicus, released in September 2007 after six
months of bottle ageing, is a smooth, classy
blend, while the Aszú 6-puttonyos 2000 is already showing its pedigree. All

the Nobilis wines de-
monstrate just what can
be achieved by smaller,
family-owned estates
with carefully chosen
terroir and skilled
winemaking.

THE WINERY WELCO-
MES VISITORS by ap-
pointment and sells
directly to the public, as
well as to restaurants in
Budapest and Paris.

TOKAJBOR-BENE

MIHÁLY BENE started his ten-hectare family estate in 1998 before his untimely death in a motor accident. His daughter, Dr. Zsuzsanna Bene, took over the management of the company and the modern winery with its 150-year-old cellars close to the centre of Bodrogkeresztúr, and has made some excellent wines following the traditional methods of her father.

THE VINEYARD PLOTS, in six different neighbourhood First Growths (such as Lapis, Dereszla and Szepsy), are planted with Furmint, Hárslevelű and Yellow Muscat.

Tokajbor-Bene
3916 Bodrogkeresztúr, Felső út 50
T: +36 47 396 017
tokajbor-bene@secnet.hu
www.tokajbor-bene.hu
Directions: From Tokaj take Road 38 to the centre of Bodrogkeresztúr and turn left onto Felső út.

THE LATE-HARVEST FURMINT and Yellow Muscat wines are well-made, clean, crisp and balanced. However, we were fascinated by the 2000 Aszú 6-puttonyos because its oxidative characteristics did not interfere with the fruit, but seemed to accentuate and enhance it.

THE WINERY ALSO PRODUCED a superb 2000 Tokaji Eszencia. How we wish these wonderful wines were within our price range for more frequent enjoyment. No wonder they were so eagerly sought-after by the rich and famous!

PUKLUS WINERY

THE PUKLUS FAMILY is renowned for its winemaking history in Bodrogkeresztúr. Their 15-hectare estate includes excellent sites in the Szentkereszt, Lapis, Dereszla and Várhegy vineyards. Furmint grows in the Lapis and Szentkereszt,

where there are also five hectares of Yellow Muscat and some of the old Gober variety; Hárslevelű dominates their plantings in the Várhegy; and Furmint and Kövérszőlő reign in the Dereszla. Family patriarch János, the chief winemaker at Kővágó, is one of the most experienced winemakers in

Tokaj, so it is hardly surprising that his sons produce accomplished late-harvest and Aszú wines that have won the admiration of international judges.

THE PUKLUS WINERY fits neatly into one of the long, traditional Hungarian farmhouses that are a prevailing

Puklus Winery
3916 Bodrogkeresztúr, Tarcali utca 13
T: +36 47 396 063
F: +36 47 396 001
puklusbor@puklusbor.hu
www.puklusbor.hu
Directions: From Tokaj take Road 38 into the centre of Bodrogkeresztúr and turn left onto Tarcali utca. Look out for a gleaming vintage motorcycle in the winery forecourt.

feature of the region. Visitors are warmly welcomed by appointment. The family is developing an adjacent property as a panzió and visitor reception area, and will be able to welcome larger numbers of visitors from 2008.

HUDACSKÓ

LIKE MANY OTHER VINTNER families in the region, the Hudacskó clan has quietly developed their wines over the last 17 years and now proudly enter them in international competitions, where their qualities have been recognised with some notable awards.

OF THE 15 HECTARES HARVESTED, nine are in the Lapis and a further three in Várhegy classified vineyards. Furmint dominates the plantings supported by Hárslevelű and a small amount of Yellow Muscat. Katalin Hudacskó, who makes the wines, loves working with Furmint from nyirok soils because of its fruitiness and very fine acids.

Hudacskó
3917 Bodrogkisfalud, Klapka út 35
T: +36 47 396 736
info@hudacsko-pince.hu
www.hudacsko-pince.hu
Directions: From Tokaj continue through Bodrogkeresztúr on Road 38 for about 3km to Bodrogkisfalud. Turn left into Klapka út at the Hudacskó sign. The winery is 1,500 metres on the left.

THE KEY TO THE HUDACSKÓ success has been lower yields with greater concentration of fruit. The Aszú/Aszú-Eszencia wines in 1999, 2000 and 2002 were quite brilliant. We also admired the softer style of her 2006 late-harvest Yellow Muscat with its elder-flower nose, and the beautifully vinified 2003 late-harvest Furmint that, intriguingly, had a hint of blackberry on the nose.

KATALIN HUDACSKÓ offered her late-harvest Furmint with really fresh, country-made goat cheese on homemade brown bread – a marriage made in heaven!

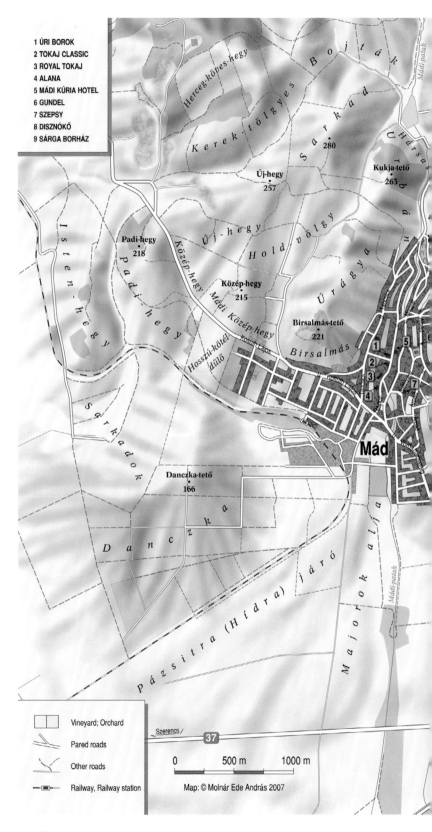

1 ÚRI BOROK
2 TOKAJ CLASSIC
3 ROYAL TOKAJ
4 ALANA
5 MÁDI KÚRIA HOTEL
6 GUNDEL
7 SZEPSY
8 DISZNÓKŐ
9 SÁRGA BORHÁZ

Vineyard; Orchard

Pared roads

Other roads

Railway, Railway station

Map: © Molnár Ede András 2007

0   500 m   1000 m

Szerencs / 37

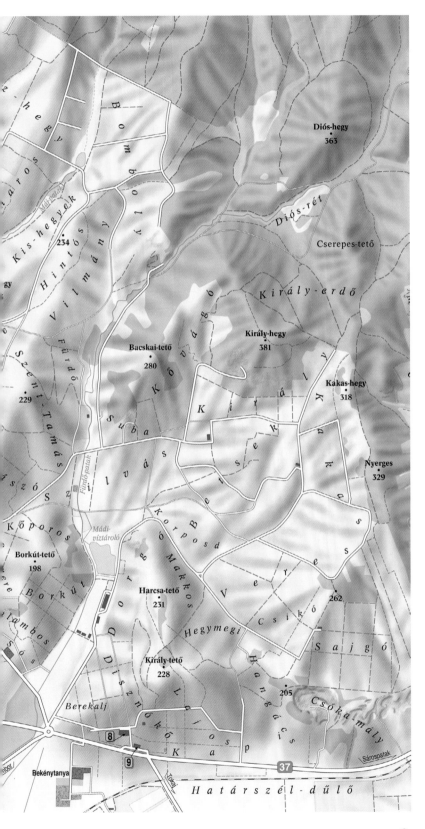

Mád Basin

THE MÁD BASIN has quite different soils to those of Tokaj Hill. They are essentially clay, more often than not mixed with broken-down rocks and minerals such as zeolite and quartz. The multilayered soils in the Mád Basin reflect the volcanic past and the long period when it was a seabed.

MÁD WAS ONCE the trading centre for Tokaji wines. Buyers came from all over Europe to select wines and arrange for their payment and shipment. The town still has many important wineries and is a gateway to the other important small towns of Tállya and Abaújszántó.

ATTRACTIONS IN MÁD

MÁD IS A PEACEFUL, provincial town and a good base for exploring the picturesque Hernád Valley – once the main wine-trading route to Poland and the Baltic Sea ports.

THE NEWLY REFURBISHED Baroque-style synagogue (re-opened in May 2004) is a testament to the importance of the Jewish contribution to the success of Tokaji wine trading in the 18th and 19th centuries. First opened in 1790, some 50 years before Budapest's Great Synagogue was built, the Mád synagogue was closed in 1944 after the entire Jewish community was forcibly carried across the border to concentration camps.

THE SYNAGOGUE is open to visitors who first call Barnabás Fehér (+36 47 348 043) or stop by Rákóczi utca 73 in Mád. Guests will find that the original interior and hand-washing basin have been restored, and there is also a poignant record of the names of those Mád Holocaust victims who were never to return.

THE MOST SPECTACULAR attraction for the bibulous traveller is the vineyard vista that can be seen from the ridge of Szent Tamás Hill. From there you will see most of the greatest vineyards of the Mád Basin. It is a 20-minute walk from the centre of Mád, or a shorter bumpy ride if you have four-wheel-drive vehicle. Ask for directions from your hotel or panzió.

ONCE UP ON THE RIDGE FACING EAST, with your Companion in hand, you should be able to identify Bomboly Vineyard just below the tree line to your left. Turning your gaze gently eastward to the old zeolite quarry, you will see the great Király Vineyard immediately beside and below it. Betsek stretches across the Basin floor, and is bounded on the far side by Kakas on

the left and Veres on the right. The red-clay soils of Szent Tamás in front of you are easily recognisable. To the right Nyulászó spreads itself lazily around the southern end of Szent Tamás Hill, while the higher slopes of Disznókő can be seen in the distance.

BEHIND YOU on the westerly hill above Mád is the thin-soiled and stony Úrágya; Sarkad is sited just above the man-made lake that catches excess water off the steep slopes.

A WALK UP THE WESTERN HILLS is rewarded with views across to Szerencs and Monok, the birthplace of Lajos Kossuth (1802-1894), the revolutionary writer who became one of the foremost politicians of his day and leader of Hungary's 1848-49 War of Independence. The Kossuth Memorial Museum in Monok is open 10:00-16:00 daily except Mondays.

MONOK WAS ALSO the home of Count Gyula Andrássy (1823-90), the first Hungarian prime minister following the Compromise of 1867 with Austria. The Count was active in the Tokaj trade. Like Kossuth, his name has been given to many streets in Hungary, the most famous of which is the boulevard leading up to Heroes' Square in Budapest.

THE PURE, clean air of the Hernád Valley is a tonic for all city dwellers. A bicycle track runs through peach and apricot orchards, past the 13th-century Boldogkő Castle and on through the Zemplén forests. To reach it from Mád take Road 38 north through Tállya before picking up the signs for the designated bikeway. The visual attraction of the valley, its stillness and its refreshingly gentle airstream foster relaxation.

ACCOMMODATIONS IN MÁD

MÁDI KÚRIA

This four-star hotel stands foursquare on the main street in the centre of Mád, as befits the former bank building that was at the heart of this once-great wine-trading town. The building has been completely renovat-

ed and redesigned as a 24-room hotel with conference facilities and an excellent provincial restaurant.

The bedrooms are large and well-furnished with good-sized bathrooms, generous cupboard space, air conditioning, television, and broadband Internet connections. Ample car parking is available at the rear of the hotel and staff are welcoming and helpful. Most of the major wineries are within a two-minute walk of the hotel.

Mádi Kúria
3909 Mád, 48 Rákóczi utca
T: +36 47 548 401
info@madkuria.hu
www.madikuria.hu

Sós has its own hectare of vines and encourages guests who are keen to try their hand at harvesting to join the picking team during the autumn season.

SÓS BORHÁZ PANZIÓ

This large guesthouse is very visible on Road 37 between Disznókő Winery and Mád. It has 11 good-sized bedrooms and a restaurant that serves appetising local fare with traditional-style Tokaji wines.

Sós Borház Panzió
3909 Mád, Near Road 37
between Tokaj and
Szerencs
T: +36 47 369 139
F: +36 47 569 018
sosborhaz@sosborhaz.hu
www.sosborhaz.hu

We liked the fact that the guesthouse is in open countryside within a 30-minute walk of some of the region's greatest vineyards, and a gentle stroll away from a small lake used by fishermen and swimmers in summer.

In Mád there are two smaller panziós. Erzsébet Vendégház (3910 Mád, Deák Ferenc utca 10, T: +36 20 932 9818) has two spotlessly clean bedrooms and an apartment furnished in rustic style. The newly renovated panzió offers clean, modestly priced accommodation. Borbarát Vendégház (3910 Mád, Magyar utca 65, T: 36 47 348 320) is known as the 'Friends of Wine Guesthouse' because that is exactly what it is. The low-cost accommodation is popular with groups of young wine enthusiasts who don't need the comparative luxury of a hotel. Its two big rooms can sleep as many as eight people, making it ideal for groups on a budget. German is spoken.

DINING IN MÁD

MÁDI KÚRIA HOTEL RESTAURANT

The premier restaurant in town, where the pleasant ambiance, varied menu, and excellent wine list are well supported by an attentive waitstaff. We liked the opportunity to buy all Gundel wines by the glass in the restaurant and buy bottles to take home at cellar-door prices. The wine list also features many of the best local wineries, including Szepsy, Royal Tokaj, Disznókő, Gábor Orosz, Tokaj Classic, and Úri Borok.

Mádi Kúria Hotel Restaurant
3909 Mád, Rákóczi utca 48
T: +36 47 548 400

The restaurant menu is strong on fish, with local catfish specialities and the richly textured angler fish ideal for matching with dry Furmints.

SÁRGA BORHÁZ (YELLOW WINE HOUSE)

The Yellow Wine House is easily found at Disznókő Winery on Road 37 as you enter the Tokaji region. The eatery describes itself as a *csárda* ('country inn') rather than a restaurant. We liked the shaded alfresco dining facilities

Sárga Borház (Yellow Wine House)
Disznókő Winery
T: +36 47 369 029
www.sargaborhaz.hu

and the good portions of well-prepared country fare offered with a good selection of wines by the glass. The superb location and ample car parking facilities makes it an excellent rendezvous point.

MIHÁLY HOLLÓKŐI WINERY AND RESTAURANT

Tállya is a 20-minute drive north of Mád on Road 38, and to reach the Hollókői restaurant take the first right into Bocskai utca some 300 metres after entering the town.

Mihály Hollókői Winery and Restaurant
3910 Tállya, 10 Bocskai utca
T: +36 47 398 054

This restaurant and winery attracts more visitors than any other in Tokaji. It is a rustic-style inn that has good alfresco dining facilities and it can accommodate large parties who come to taste wine at the geometric centre of Europe.

WINERIES

DISZNÓKŐ

DISZNÓKŐ HAS always been a prized estate. The Rákóczi Family owned it in the 1600s, followed by prominent aristocrats Melchior de Lónyay in the 1700s and Baron de Waldbott in the 1800s. Now it belongs to AXA Mille-

simes, a giant French insurance company that owns a string of fine-wine properties, including Chateau Pichon-Longueville Baron in Bordeaux, Chateau Suduiraut in Sauternes, and Quinta do Noval in Oporto.

THE ESTATE is superbly sited on south-facing slopes alongside Road 37 to Sárospatak at the entrance to the Tokaji region.

THE OWNERS HAVE USED it imaginatively to express their confidence in the future of Tokaj. They commissioned Dezső Ekler, one of Hungary's very best modern architects, to design a completely new winery with a gravity-fed production line and an attractive, curved viewing gallery that allows visitors to see the whole production process at harvest time.

EKLER HAS ALSO RESTORED the old press house, which now serves as a relaxing restaurant appropriately named Sárga Borház or Yellow Wine House; he also designed what must be the wine world's most attractive tractor shed, a building inspired by the yurts (round tent-like structures) of the original Magyars.

ABOVE THE WINERY is a splendid viewing platform next to the rock shaped like a huge wild boar, from which the winery takes its name. The platform offers a view of the whole estate, with the celebrated Kapi Vineyard away to your left on the lower-middle part of the slope.

WHEN AXA acquired the property in 1992 they began replanting the whole estate at a density of 4,500 vines per hectare, with a low-cordon training system designed to increase the rate and extent of botrytisation.

Disznókő
3910 Tokaj, Pf 10
T: +36 47 569 410
F: +36 47 369 138
disznoko@disznoko.hu
www.disznoko.hu
Directions: 10km north of Tokaj on Road 38; 10km east of Szerencs on Road 37 towards Sárospatak. The winery and the Yellow Wine House restaurant are clearly visible from the road.
Owners: AXA Millesimes (France)
Estate Area: 130ha, 100ha under vine planted at a density of 4,500 vines per hectare on a low cordon.
Varieties planted: Furmint 60%, Hárslevelű 30%, Yellow Muscat 5%, Zéta 5%
Tour and tasting cost: From Ft 2,500
Visiting hours: 10:00-17:00

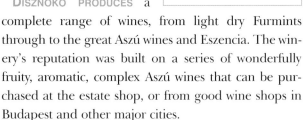

DISZNÓKŐ PRODUCES a complete range of wines, from light dry Furmints through to the great Aszú wines and Eszencia. The winery's reputation was built on a series of wonderfully fruity, aromatic, complex Aszú wines that can be purchased at the estate shop, or from good wine shops in Budapest and other major cities.

DISZNÓKŐ WINES HAVE won the admiration of Hungarian and international wine writers and judges, and have brought home a host of gold medals from major international competitions. We highly recommend their winery tour because it provides an excellent introduction to the region and its wines.

THERE ARE VARIOUS TASTING programmes from which to choose and after sampling you can visit the winery shop to select the bottles you wish to take home. The Yellow Wine House has recently refurbished its pleasant alfresco dining facilities and is a splendid place to take lunch or dinner.

KAPI VINEYARD

Disznókő is the name of the estate, but Kapi is the name given to its most celebrated vine-yard area. What makes the Kapi so special? It is a south-facing slope protected from the cold-est winds, where the well-drained clay soil provides a natural home for the Furmint. Furmint provides a wonderful structure for Aszú wines, but in the Kapi its very fine acids prevent the high residual sugar of the aszu berries from becoming too cloying. The clay topsoil con-tributes to the aroma and flavour of the wine, but its character is determined by the rhyolite bedrock that provides the essential nutrients to imbue the wine with its own special identity. At around 100-150 metres above sea level Kapi is well-positioned to attract botrytisation. In the great vintage of 1999 this vineyard produced an exceptional wine, one of the finest Aszú 6-puttonyos wines we have tasted.

Range of Wines

DRY FURMINT Made from old vines on the western slopes of the estate and fermented in stainless steel, the wine is left on its lees for a month to gain additional flavour before being bottled in the spring following the vintage. Ideally it should be kept for 6-9 months in bottle before drinking with seafood, caviar, or poultry.

SWEET SZAMORODNI Made from bunches of botrytised and non-botrytised grapes, it makes a sophisticated aperitif that fills the mouth with fine flavours.

LATE-HARVEST Its freshness and fruit-filled flavours are enticing and make it an ideal wine for pure relaxation and enjoyment.

ASZÚ 3-, 4-, 5-, AND 6-PUTTONYOS Made only with the best handpicked aszu berries and matured in oak for a minimum of two years and in bottle for 12 months. Offers rich aromas and complex flavours best enjoyed with rich foods, such as *pate de fois gras* and ripe Roquefort cheese.

TOKAJ ESSENCIA 1993 Nectar of the gods. Matured in oak for ten years with a further three years of bottle ageing before release in 2006. This exceptional wine has 425 g/l residual sugar, 11 degrees acidity and 24% dry extract. It could last for 100 years or more.

ROYAL TOKAJI WINE COMPANY

THE ROYAL TOKAJ WINE Company was the first of the new companies to be for-med (even before the regime change of 1989), as a direct result of the enthusiasm of a group of foreign investors led by Peter Vinding-Diers and Hugh Johnson.

VINDING-DIERS, representing Danish interests, persuaded Johnson, the doyen of the world's wine writers, to back his efforts to revive one of the

The Royal Tokaji Wine Company
3909 Mád, Rákóczi út 35
T: +36 47 348 011
F: +36 47 348 359
royal-tokaji@royal-tokaji.hu
www.royal-tokaji.com
London Sales Office:
sales@royal-tokaji.com
Directions: From Disznókő take Road 38 north to Mád. Turn right at the traffic lights for the town centre. The winery, clearly signed, is on the left.
Owner: Royal Tokaji Wine Company Ltd
Estate: 110ha under vine at a density of 5,000 vines/ha on a low cordon
Varieties planted: Furmint 70%, Hárslevelű 25%, Yellow Muscat 5%
Tour and tasting cost: From Ft 2,500

world's truly original and great white wines, all but forgotten over the previous 50 years.

THEY WERE inspired to make their investment after tasting what Johnson described as "a wine that would make angels sing out loud in praise" – an Aszú 6-puttonyos made by István Szepsy.

VINDING-DIERS persuaded a group of 62 small growers to sell a hectare of their classified vineyard land to the joint venture in return for shares in the Royal Tokaji Company that would make and market the wines. Thus the growers would provide the grapes while the investors would build a modern winery and take the wines into world markets.

FROM THE OUTSET ROYAL TOKAJ decided to concentrate on producing single-vineyard wines made from the top vineyards of Mézes Mály, Nyulászó, Szent Tamás and Betsek. It was a bold and imaginative decision, and its purpose was to remind wine lovers that Tokaj was, with Burgundy, among the first of the

world's great wine regions to recognise the importance of terroir. It was also a statement of belief that Tokaji's finest vineyards justified positioning alongside the Great Growths of Burgundy and Bordeaux.

THE JOINTLY-OWNED vineyards were replanted, pruned, and trained to produce lower yields of the riper, healthier, botrytised grapes needed to make exceptional wines.

ROYAL DECIDED to make its wines in the traditional manner, with greater extraction and longer barrel-ageing, during which gentle and controlled oxidation of the wine was permitted in the same way that it had been for centuries, adding colour, aroma, and complexity to the wine.

MODERN TASTES DEMAND FRESHER, fruitier Aszú wines, and the better Tokaji winemakers, such as Károly Áts and István Turóczi, have learned how to combine traditional virtues with modern technology in the Royal Tokaj range of wines, which extends from dry Furmint through to the great single-vineyard Aszú wines like Mézes Mály.

ROYAL HAS INVESTED MORE in its vineyards and worldwide marketing programmes than in bricks and mortar, so do not expect great architecture when you visit their winery in the centre of Mád. Nevertheless, visitors are

warmly welcomed to the former Diocesan Bishop's residence with its pleasant courtyard featuring a bronze bust of Hugh Johnson.

THE COMPANY OFFERS a series of tasting programmes to visitors by appointment. Having tasted the Royal range of wines we recommend you to ask for directions up St. Tamás Hill opposite the winery, where you can look down on the First Growth vineyards of the Mád Basin – Szent Tamás, Nyulászó and Betsek – from whence Royal Tokaj's single-vineyard wines come.

Range of Wines

DRY FURMINT 2005 Full-bodied dry white wine. Half the production is barrel-fermented and aged in oak for five months before being blended with the other half made in stainless steel.

THE ÁTS CUVEE 2005 An outstanding late-harvest wine made from mixed bunches of all three of the main varieties, vinified in stainless steel before being racked into wood for about six months and bottle-matured for a further six months.

ROYAL ASZÚ 5-PUTTONYOS 2000 Made from the finest aszú berries and matured in cask for two or three years before further aging in bottle. Its prominent fruit flavours make it an attractive and popular wine.

BETSEK FIRST GROWTH ASZÚ 6-PUTTONYOS 1999 The bouquet is appealing – well-botrytised grapes with a dried apricot flavour. The high acidity restrains the 185 g/l sugar, and a hint of peppermint adds freshness to this excellent example of the vintage that was awarded a Decanter Gold Medal.

NYULÁSZÓ FIRST GROWTH ASZÚ 6-PUTTONYOS 1999 Wonderful nutty and apricot aromas that unfold gradually. A rich and heady wine from a great vintage.

SZENT TAMÁS FIRST GROWTH ASZÚ 6-PUTTONYOS 1999 Straw-pale colour. Rich fruit balanced with wonderfully fine acids. A fine and elegant wine from a memorable vintage.

MÉZES MÁLY GREAT GROWTH ASZÚ 6-PUTTONYOS 1999 Luscious honey-rich wine that fills the mouth with complex flavours. A classic wine with great charm and extraordinary length that lingers in the senses.

TOKAJI ESSENCIA 1999 The most remarkable nectar produced by the winery. The first-ever wine to be awarded 100 points by the Wine & Spirit International tasting panel. The judges agreed that the wine had everything – great aroma, body, poise, finesse, elegance and length. Such perfection does not come cheap, but if you are seeking excellence or have a special anniversary in mind, then be prepared to pay around Ft 100,000 for a 50cl bottle.

MÉZES MÁLY VINEYARD

Mézes Mály is one of the two Great Growths of Tokaj. As early as the 15th century it was identified as being something special; in the 16th century it was owned by the Rákóczi Family before being taken over by the Austrian Treasury in 1713, and then the Hungarian State after 1918. When it was privatised in 1989, Royal Tokaj moved decisively to acquire eight prime hectares of mature vines in time to make their first single-vineyard wine from this Great Growth in 1993.

The vineyard is easy to identify because it lies just below the St. Terézia chapel that you will see as you drive into Tarcal, and also because there is a small, yellow-walled vineyard-workers' house in its midst, known locally as Johnson's Var or Johnson's Castle. The best parts of the vineyard are between 120-160 metres above the Tisza River and its water meadows – the ideal location for ripeness and good botrytisation.

The deep loess soil overlays the hard old volcanic rock of Tokaj Hill and produces rich, elegant wines. The name Mézes Mály translates as 'honey pot', and one sip of the 1999 Mézes Mály Great Growth Aszú 6-Puttonyos will help you understand why. It is truly a "wine fit for the table of a king," as it was described by those who shaped the 1700 classification of vineyards.

ISTVÁN SZEPSY

ISTVÁN SZEPSY, the best-known and most respected of all current Tokaji wine-growers, has devoted his life to perfecting the wines of his native region. Honoured by the President of the Republic of Hungary, admired by cus-

tomers and competitors alike, and adored by Tokaj Aszú enthusiasts, the key events in Szepsy's life are worth recording as an example of what dedicated vintners can achieve.

BORN TO ONE OF THE LEADING GROWERS IN BODROGKERESZTÚR, who died prematurely in 1970 when young István was just 19 years old, Szepsy determined to follow in his father's footsteps. Times were hard for the fatherless family. Obliged to sell the vineyards to survive, Szepsy hurried home after graduation from Budapest Horticultural

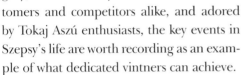

István Szepsy
3909 Mád, Batthyány utca 59
T: +36 47 348 349
F: +36 47 348 724
szepsyistvan@t-online.hu
www.szepsy.hu
Directions: Batthyány utca is almost directly behind the Mádi Kúria Hotel on the way up to St. Tamás Hill.
Owner: Szepsy Family
Estate: 62ha, 40ha under vine. The planting density and training systems vary according to the age and location of the vineyard. Both low-cordon and stake-planting methods are used where appropriate.
Varieties planted: Furmint 60%, Hárslevelű 35%, Yellow Muscat 4%, Zéta 1%
Visiting hours: Trade only by appointment.

University, taking up a job at the Mád Cooperative where he later became chief wine-maker.

IN 1976 HE RENTED a small vineyard plot and began to grow his own grapes, saving the money he earned from them until he had enough to acquire other tiny parcels of land in First Growth vineyards. In 1989 he agreed, along with 61 other growers in the cooperative, to exchange his land for shares in the Royal Tokaj joint venture company. The foreign investors, backed by the cooperative members, asked him to be their winemaker.

THE INVESTORS INVITED HIM TO BORDEAUX, where he visited Chateau d'Yquem in Sauternes for the first time. It was in the middle of that great vineyard that Szepsy resolved that he would follow his own winemaking instincts. In 1991 he made the move to set up his own winery – a brave decision for a man with a wife and three young children to support, and without any means to finance the business other than by making and selling very good wines.

SZEPSY'S EXPERIENCE with the Mád Cooperative had prepared him well for his self-appointed task. He knew exactly where to find the best botrytised grapes. He started in the Király Vineyard and gradually acquired more land with mature Furmint and Hárslevelű vines in other First Growth vineyards such as Szent Tamás, Betsek, and Nyulászó. Furmint provides the structure for his wines; Hárslevelű contributes richness of aroma and body.

OVER THE LAST 15 YEARS he has steadily built his holdings up to 62 hectares, 40 of which are under vine, and which he now works with his son, son-in-law and daughter, as well as a team of experienced and loyal workers. He plants quite densely and prunes to short spurs with one eye. After the flowering he cuts back to six or seven fruit-bearing shoots per plant and encourages the growth of smaller bunches that tend to ripen earlier and have a higher concentration of sugar. During the summer he selects the best bunches, ruthlessly pruning any that he considers to be badly formed or unlikely to botrytise well or ripen fully.

SUCH RIGOROUS WORK in the vineyard limits his production to between 400-600 litres of Aszú wine per hectare, and yet he has held to the promise he made at Chateau d'Yquem – to make the best possible wine without compromise.

SZEPSY CONSTANTLY reviews every aspect of his craft. When he started making Aszú wines he used to make his base wine from the non-botrytised grapes picked at the start of the harvest. Now he prefers must obtained from overripe (but not botrytised) grapes picked as late as possible, because they make a base wine that produces richer and more concentrated Aszús.

AFTER A SHORT MACERATION and gentle pressing, Szepsy draws off the must into barrels for fermentation. He relies on natural yeasts to start the process and makes no attempt to stop it. After fermentation he racks the wine into new 225-litre oak barrels for a minimum of ageing two years in his deep cool cellars.

WHEN THE DIFFERENT elements in the wine are harmonised he bottles his wines carefully, and gives them at least 12 months of bottle ageing before release.

SZEPSY BELIEVES in allowing nature to take its course. He is reluctant to interfere in the winemaking process, and this means that in some years his wines will have a higher level of alcohol than those of vintners who stop fermentation by chilling or by the discretionary use of sulphur dioxide.

IT IS THIS CONSIDERED, unhurried, non-interfering approach – and the attention he gives to every detail – that makes his wines so sought-after. His current range of wines is limited to a dry Furmint, Szepsy Tokaji Cuvee (a great wine in its own right), and his prized Aszú 6-puttonyos.

WHEN THE VINTAGE IS poor and he is not fully satisfied with any of the wines he has made (as in 1994 and 2001), he will sell them in bulk to other vintners. Such integrity has helped build a worldwide following for his wines despite their cost.

IN 2007 SZEPSY hopes to introduce seven new single-vineyard dry wines from his plots in the great vineyards of the Mád Basin. As he produces relatively modest quantities it would be wise to register your interest as soon as it is piqued; wines can be purchased through the Szepsy Website and from wine merchants in Budapest.

Range of Wines

DRY FURMINT SZENT TAMÁS 2005 Made from 55-year-old Furmint vines grown in multilayered volcanic soils, the wine is well-structured with firm acidity. Baked apple, brown sugar, and apricot are discernible on the nose and on the mineral-driven flavours. An elegant wine with great length.

SZEPSY TOKAJ CUVEE 2003 A superb example of late-harvest wine. Raisin, citrus, and apricot on the nose. Rich texture and good complexity. A wonderful entry point for those really interested in the purity and excellence of Szepsy's wines.

ASZÚ 6-PUTTONYOS 2002 Apricot, raisin, and dried fruit on the nose. Great structure as always with really crisp acidity to balance the 222g/l sugar. A refined, elegant wine with good length that needs time to develop fully.

KIRÁLY VINEYARD

Király ('king') is a special vineyard, as its name implies. Situated just below the old zeolite quarry in the Mád Basin, its mineral-rich topsoil overlies hard old volcanic rock.

Protected from cold northerly winds by the remains of a quarried hill, Király Vineyard's soil warms up quickly and retains its heat throughout the growing season, producing powerful wines that are the basis of many fine Aszú blends.

Almost every Tokaji grower aspires to own a plot in Király. Szepsy had the advantage of getting to know the vineyard well during his years as winemaker at the Mád Cooperative, and it was in Király that he purchased his first plot when he started again in 1991. Since then he has patiently acquired 12 more hectares of older Furmint and Hárslevelű vines in the Greater Király.

The topsoil has a reddish hue, being clay mixed with broken-down zeolite and quartz. The undersoil contains zeolite debris on top of thick clay. Underneath is hard old rock. The vine roots seek out cracks in these old rocks in their search for water and nutrients. It is those nutrients that give character and longevity to the wines made from them.

Szepsy and other owners in Király have painstakingly reclaimed and terraced the higher slopes of this great vineyard, which is expected to continue to produce exceptional wines for a long time yet.

SZENT TAMÁS VINEYARD

Szent Tamás is on a slightly higher slope with a sharper angle of incline and a more southeasterly exposure than Király. On the higher reaches the red-clay surface soil is mixed with broken rock; on the slope itself the soil is thinner, sometimes giving way to a metre-thick band of yellow clay that lies below it. Underneath there is yet another layer of broken-down zeolite with a greenish tint to it, then more clay before the rhyolite base rock. The big cracks and perforations in the rhyolite tuff allow the vine roots to penetrate to a depth of nine metres or more. The soils have a high pH factor that helps generate refined acids; soils that in some vintages produce rich, smooth, flavoursome wines, and in others produce more muscular yet elegant wines.

Apart from Szepsy the largest owners in the 50-hectare vineyard are Royal Tokaj, Úri Borok, and the Gelsey Family. But few would dispute that the most outstanding wines to date are Szepsy's 2005 Szent Tamás Dry Furmint, Royal Tokaji's Szent Tamás Aszú 6-Puttonyos 1999, and Úri Borok's 1999 Szent Tamás Cuvee. The vineyard has an extraordinary character and personality and, like Király, has become sought-after because of its consistent performance.

GUNDEL WINERY

<small>FOUNDED BY GREAT RESTAURATEUR</small> George Lang and Ronald Lauder, scion of the famous cosmetics company, Gundel is now substantially owned by Danubius Hotels under the chairmanship of Sir Bernard Schrier.

<small>THE WINERY,</small> managed by Zsolt Kálmán, owns 25 hectares in Bomboly Vineyard on the south-facing slopes above Mád where, unusually, Hárslevelű dominates the plantings with 60% and Furmint makes up the balance. The company also buys in Muscat grapes from a trusted local grower.

<small>ZSOLT KÁLMÁN</small> is an experienced winemaker who delights in the fact that every single vintage yields a wine of different character. "Tokaj is not a winemaking factory where a standard blend is produced year after year. The diversity of the vintages keeps us on our toes," he says.

Gundel Winery
3909 Mád, Árpád utca 37
T: +36 47 348 383
gundel@gundel.hu
www.gundel.hu
Owner: Danubius Hotels
Estate: 25ha under vine at a density of 5,500 vines per hectare.
Varieties planted: Hárslevelű 60%, Furmint 40%
Visiting hours: Trade visits by appointment only. Wines may be tasted and purchased at Mádi Kúria Hotel by prior arrangement.
Tour and tasting cost: From Ft 2,500
Languages spoken: English, German

THE HONEYED INFLUENCE of Hárslevelű is attractive. Its aromas and flavours combine to make charming Aszú wines that are popular with consumers and other Hungarian winemakers. When the late Tibor Gál was asked to introduce Gundel's award-winning 1993 Aszú 6-Puttonyos at a celebratory dinner, he stood up and said: "This wine is so good, you should taste it without delay," and sat down again.

MOST VISITORS LIKE to taste wine in the cellar. But the very best place to taste the Gundel range is in the Mádi Kúria restaurant where they are available by the decilitre and can be matched with the dishes you have selected.

FURTHERMORE, the restaurant offers patrons the chance to buy bottles to take home at cellar-door prices. The 1993 Aszú 6-Puttonyos must be one of the best value-for-money purchases in Hungary.

MANY OF THE WINES are also available at the Gundel restaurant in Budapest, and at the Budapest Airport shops, where the range is more limited but they also stock Gundel goose liver – an excellent complement to Aszú wines.

Range of Wines

DRY FURMINT 2005 A full-bodied and food-friendly dry Furmint with mineral strength and firm acids.

HÁRSLEVELŰ 2006 A stunning wine with a natural residual sugar content of 75g/l and glorious honeyed aromas.

DRY SZAMORODNI 2000 A classic wine matured in small casks for 37 months before being bottled in 2004. Giuseppe Vaccarini, President of the Guild of Sommeliers, described it as the paradigm for all those trying to vinify this special wine so admired by gourmets.

LATE-HARVEST MUSCAT 2001 One of the first wineries to introduce this style after 1990, Gundel was advised on its vinification by near-neighbour István Szepsy. An elegant and luscious wine with crisp acids.

ASZÚ 6-PUTTONYOS 1993 Superb vintage. Deep golden colour, expansive aromas and wonderfully generous flavours that open out in the glass. Excellent value for money.

BOMBOLY VINEYARD

Bomboly is easily recognizable because it sits high on the hill (as its name 'open hill' implies) above Mád just below the tree line. It is a southwest-facing vineyard with clay soil mixed with rhyolite and andesite rocks, which accounts for its full-bodied wines with strong mineral character. The wines have a long finish and good ageing potential.

Hárslevelű dominates the plantings, and it is easy to understand why when you taste the luscious 2006 vintage wines. Their rich aroma and fruit flavours are well-supported by fine acids. Furmint adds firmer acids to the Aszú blends, and its fresh fruit marries well with its sister variety.

In most years the wines undergo a completely natural malolactic fermentation that has the effect of intensifying the aromas and flavours, and softening the wine to make it a delight to drink with or without food.

PENDITS

THIS PRIVATELY-OWNED ESTATE, run by Márta Wille-Baumkauff, takes its name from the First Growth vineyard that the family reclaimed from forest and thick undergrowth. The winery also owns vineyard plots in Király at Mád and at

Pendits
3881 Abaújszántó, Béke utca 111
T & F: +36 47 330 567
pendits@axelero.hu
www.pendits.com
Directions: Follow Road 38 up the Hernád Valley to the southern outskirts of Abaújszántó. The winery is in the cellar row on the right.
Owner: Márta Wille-Baumkauff
Estate: 20ha, 13ha under vine planted at a density of 5,500-7,000 vines per hectare on a low cordon pruned to one bud with 1-2 clusters per shoot.
Varieties planted: Furmint 80%, Hárslevelű 15%, Yellow Muscat 5%
Visiting hours: Telephone or e-mail for appointments. The Pendits Vineyard is about a ten-minute walk from the cellar.

Tarcal, where the vines are pruned to one bud with a restricted number of bunches per vine. This low-yield policy has paid off with some stylish dry Furmint, late-harvest and Aszú wines.

MÁRTA, AS SHE IS affectionately known in the trade, is one of the many accomplished women winemakers in Tokaj, but is the only one we know that is actively involved in working her vineyards. She is a self-taught horticulturalist and vintner who developed her skills by practising them, while graciously acknowledging advice and encouragement from master winemakers István Szepsy and Egon Müller.

THE FIRST TOKAJI WINE grower to practice organic viticulture, Márta is committed to being fully biodynamic by 2010. Since the sad loss of her hus-

band to cancer, Márta's greatest solace is to take her dog for an evening walk in the beautiful vineyard that they restored together.

MÁRTA'S COURAGE and tenacity have been rewarded by increased sales of her stylish and innovative wines to merchants and restaurants in Germany and Switzerland. We heartily recommend making an appointment to visit her terraced vineyards, where she has fashioned a delightful outdoor tasting area surrounded by roses and almond trees that offer superb views across the Hernád Valley.

Range of Wines

FURMINT AND HÁRSLEVELŰ BLEND 2006 Superbly crafted with delicious fresh-fruit flavours and keen acidity.

FURMINT AND YELLOW MUSCAT BLEND 2005 Delightful example of what the winery does best – find interesting grape flavours and vinify them well.

BOTRYTIS SELECTION 2001 A wine made from 100% botrytised Furmint grapes carefully selected on the vine and again on the sorting tray at the winery. Made in the same way as an Aszú, but not aged for the full two years because Márta wants to keep the fruit fresh and stabilised. It is a genuinely noble late-harvest wine that is a favourite with the restaurant trade.

ASZÚ 6-PUTTONYOS 2000 Bouquet of freshly gathered raisins and young fruit with a delightfully smooth and silky finish.

ASZÚ-ESZENCIA 2000 Remarkably pale in colour, yet with all the concentration of fruit and flavour we expect from such a fine wine.

TOKAJ CLASSIC

IN 1993, András Bruhács and two fellow classical musicians decided to add a string to their bow by jointly investing in a Tokaj winery, which they appropriately renamed Tokaj Classic.

THEY TOOK GOOD advice and acquired eight hectares in the First Growth Király and Betsek vineyards, and appointed local winemaker Imre Galambosi to manage the vineyards and make their wines.

THEIR JUDGEMENT HAS PROVEN SOUND. For six consecutive years Tokaj Classic has won a gold medal for its Aszú 6-Puttonyos at the London International Wine & Spirit Competition. This is a unique achievement and demonstrates the value of focusing attention on a limited range of wines and putting the winery's whole effort behind them.

Tokaj Classic
3909 Mád, Rákóczi utca 45
T & F: +36 47 348 201
T: +49 611 957 0873 (Export Office, Wiesbaden, Germany)
bruhacs@tokaj-classic.com
www.tokaj-classic.com
Directions: Mád town centre. Rákóczi utca is next door to Royal Tokaj Winery.

AS ONE WOULD expect from a company called Classic, the Aszú wines are made in the traditional style, though with modern technology.

ENCOURAGED BY THEIR success and customer demand, Classic has added a dry Furmint and Late Harvest Classic Cuvee to its range.

TOKAJ CLASSIC is an active supporter of Tokaj Renaissance. "Tokaj is an unpolished diamond," Bruhács explains, "and our ambition is to make it sparkle." He admits that his love of music has made him a romantic, and that dreaming of the golden wines of Tokaj has inspired his interpretations of Mahler, Mozart and Wagner. The Hungarian cellist, married to a charming American, is based in Wiesbaden but returns to Tokaj whenever he can.

IN THE MEANTIME, Galambosi maintains the high standard of winemaking that earned the winery its collection of gold medals. Hungarian distribution is handled by In Vino Veritas; exports are handled through the Wiesbaden office. Sales have been made to the USA, UK, Germany and Holland.

Range of Wines

DRY FURMINT 2005 Straw-pale and full-bodied, this wine is a true son of the Mádi soils.

LATE-HARVEST 2005 Well-selected bunches of partly botrytised grapes emphasise the aromas and flavours.

ASZÚ 6-PUTTONYOS 1999 This award-winning wine is made in the traditional style with modern technology. Its lovely deep colour is matched with a full range of enticing aromas and the rich taste lingers long in the mouth.

ALANA-TOKAJ

ATTILA NÉMETH, who made his reputation while raising the profile of his family winery in the Mátra region, has now turned his attention to crafting artisanal wines from Tokaji terroirs.

IN 2005 Németh Family interests in Hungary and the USA purchased the 21-hectare Lowenstein Estate, bringing their total holding to 22.5 hectares, most of which is in Király, Betsek and Veres vineyards in the heart of the Mád Basin.

NÉMETH HAS BEEN making small-batch fermentations to assess the potential of each of the different plots that the family purchased, most of which are planted with older Furmint and Hárslevelű vines. Where he has to replant he is selecting clones of those varieties that will produce smaller grapes with an even greater concentration of fruit.

COMMITTED TO MAKING top-quality wines, Németh operates strict yield control and is keen to develop eco-friendly production methods. He is patiently working his way through experimental stages before releasing his first Aszú wines, which makes his winery even more interesting than usual to visit because he is willing to share his thought processes.

IN THE MEANTIME he has demonstrated his winemaking prowess with a stylish Hárslevelű and a late-harvest Yellow Muscat from Betsek. The first is aromatic and bold; the second a fresh, vibrant wine with tingling acidity.

Both wines can be sampled in the temporary tasting room at Rákóczi út 15 while the adjoining manor house is being renovated to become a modern winery and visitor-reception area. The new winery is expected to be ready to make wines from the 2007 harvest.

THE FAMILY, whose Márta wines are well-known in Hungary, has established trading links in the USA.

Alana-Tokaj
3909 Mád, Rákóczi út 15
T: +36 20 954 2772 (mobile)
alana_tokaj@yahoo.com
Directions: From Tokaj take Road 38 north to the traffic lights at Mád and turn right to the town centre.
Owner: Attila and András Németh and family
Estate: 21ha in Király, Betsek and Veres; 1.5ha in Tolcsva

BODVIN

WHEN HE HEARD that plots in First Growth Tokaji vineyards were being privatised, USA resident Géza Bodnár hurried

Bodvin
3909 Mád, Ságvári utca 3
T: +36 47 348 785
F: +36 47 348 785

home to Hungary to acquire ten hectares in Király, Betsek and Veres vineyards and asked Gábor Orosz, his brother-in-law, to look after them and make his wines.

OROSZ, A GIFTED VINTNER, produces the Bodvin wines in a different style than those of his own winery. The 2006 tank-fermented varietal wines we tasted were made to a very high standard. We particularly liked the Bodvin 2005 Kings Hill Dry Furmint, vinified with flair and imagination.

THE BODVIN ASZÚ-ESZENCIA 1993 has been highly praised, and is much sought-after on the US market. The Bodnárs are active members of Tokaj Renaissance. The family made a shrewd choice of vineyard plots and an excellent choice of winemaker.

Úri Borok
3909 Mád, Rákóczi utca 65
T: +36 47 348 601
uriborok@axelero.hu
www.uriborok.hu
Directions: The cellar is on Rákóczi utca in the centre of Mád.
Owners: Vince and Szilvia Gergely
Estate: 16ha, of which 14ha are under vine. Planting density varies depending on vineyard and age of the vines.
Varieties planted: Furmint, Hárslevelű, and Yellow Muscat
Tour and tasting cost: From Ft 3,000
Visiting times: 10:00-17:00

ÚRI BOROK

THE NAME OF THE WINERY translates as Noble Wines, and Vince Gergely and his wife Szilvia maintain a very high standard of quality in keeping with their winery name. They own ten

hectares, most of which are on the south-facing slopes of Szent Tamás in Mád; and the balance in the nearby Danczka and in loess soil at Tarcal.

ÚRI BOROK WAS one of the original members of the Mád Circle, a group of the region's winemakers who committed themselves in the early 1990s to making the best possible Aszú wines.

THE QUALITY of his grapes is more important to Gergely than modern technology. He prefers to make his wines from older Furmint and Hárslevelű vines, although he uses Yellow Muscat in the preparation of his fermenting must for soaking the hand-

picked aszú berries. The result is rich and generous wines with great purity of flavour.

Úri Borok wines are aged in a charming underground cellar network, parts of which date back to the 13th century. The cellar, once owned by Baron Orczy (whose daughter Emmuska wrote *The Scarlet Pimpernel*) has been sensitively restored, and recent additions to the visitor-reception facilities have made it an excellent winery to visit. Up to 60 people can be accommodated at once, and three different tasting programmes are offered.

Range of Wines

Dry Furmint 2000 Aged in the barrel for two and a half years, the wine has a whiff of the oxidative as intended, but offers rich fruit flavours and good length. It is a wine that shows the basic strength of Tokaji Furmint and its ability to last well.

Furmint Semisweet 2004 With 25 grams per litre of residual sugar, and butter-melon and sweet apple tones, this is a delightful semisweet version of Furmint.

Muskotály Late-Harvest 2005 Litchi and elderberry dominate the bouquet while firm acidity balances 60g/l sugar, making a delightful example of this variety and style.

Szent Tamás Cuvée 2002 A superb orange colour and 151 g/l of residual sugar, along with caramel and ginger tastes, make it attractive.

Aszú 6-Puttonyos 1999 An orgy of flavours. Dried fruits, Christmas-cake icing, and marzipan on top of apricot. A richly flavoured wine that reveals the pride and joy of its makers.

GÁBOR OROSZ

A HIGHLY TRAINED OENOLOGIST, Gábor Orosz started his winemaking career at Gundel. Since 2000 he has made his own wines from eight prime hectares in the Király, Betsek and Veres First Growth vineyards.

OROSZ USES his skill and imagination to produce interesting wines, such as a superbly balanced late-harvest Furmint with 12 g/l residual sugar. In 2006 he picked his best, sun-kissed Hárslevelű grapes for another noble late-harvest wine that is already showing the qualities of a very classy libation.

IT WAS A REAL PLEASURE to accompany Orosz among the vines he loves and maintains so well, and to with him visit the small house in Nyulászó Vineyard from which his grandfather kept a close eye on his vines on sun-drenched evenings. When questioned about the greatest influence on his winemaking, Orosz replied that he felt that viniculture was his blood legacy, in his DNA – hardly surprising when five generations of the family have tended vines on the slopes around Mád.

DURING OUR VISIT OROSZ received news of winning a Gold Medal for his Aszú 6-Puttonyos 2000 at the Challenge International du Vin. We enjoyed a glass of the same in celebration and determined to keep in touch with this quiet and unassuming son of the soil who treasures his native vineyards so dearly.

> **Gábor Orosz**
> 3909 Mád, Táncsics utca 4
> T: +36 47 348 076
> **Directions:** Office in Táncsics utca parallel with Rákóczi utca, near the centre of Mád.

OTHER GROWERS IN THE MÁD BASIN

MÁD, TÁLLYA AND ABAÚJSZÁNTÓ are home to a number of excellent yet small family wineries. In Mád many of them can be found on Tancsis utca, which runs parallel to Rákóczi utca. There you will find:

LENKEY

THE WINERY was founded in 1999 with ten hectares in First Growth vineyards around Mád such as Úrágya, Szent Tamás, Nyulászó, Betsek and Bomboly. The grapes from each plot are blended to

> **Lenkey**
> 3909 Mád, Táncsics utca 29-31
> T: +36 47 548 056 F: +36 47 548 057
> Budapest, Esze Tamás utca 68
> T: +36 30 962 7332 (mobile)

make Kis Családom ('My Little Family') Cuvee. The wines made by Miklós Takács are fruity and elegant, and can be tasted in the cellar by appointment.

MONYÓK

JÓZSEF AND NORBERT MONYÓK own 12 hectares in First Growth vineyards such as
Nyulászó, Király, Betsek and Úrágya, but also buy in grapes from other growers. It is an enterprising company that exports 84% of its production to major
markets around the world and is looking to expand production. We tasted the
fruity 2005 late-harvest Cuvee in the deep cellar opposite the family house,
from where the balance of production is sold.

> **Monyók**
> 3909 Mád, Táncsics utca 18
> T: +36 47 548 033

TÖRÖK

BÉLA TÖRÖK established his family winery with six hectares, and now has ten.
He is yet another example of a small vintner making excellent wines from
good growths. We admired his open-
minded and refreshing approach to
winemaking, and the sound technique
practised in the late-harvest Yellow Muscat and Hárslevelű wines we tasted.

> **Török**
> 3909 Mád, Táncsics utca
> T: +36 47 363 835, +36 30 269 1002
> torokpince.mad@freemail.hu

AUREUM (FORMERLY COLOR, ODOR, SAPOR)

FOUNDED IN 1998 with six hectares in Nyulászó and Betsek, and another seven
hectares being replanted in the Kakas Vineyard, the company offers a well-
made range of wines for
sampling at its tasting
rooms in central downtown
Budapest. The shop sells
the range at very reason-
able prices.

> **Aureum**
> 3909 Mád, Árpád utca 33/b
> T: +36 47 378 780 F: +36 47 348 360
> Head Office: 1056 Budapest, Belgrád rakpart 19
> T: +36 1 483 1904, +36 1 483 1456 (wine shop)
> F: +36 1 483 1905

PROMONTOBOR

ALMOST THE EXACT opposite of the small family wineries in Mád,
Promontobor is a large and successful wine trading company that frequent-
ly buys and blends surplus wines from
other wineries and exports them in large
quantities at competitive prices. This
winery is perhaps of greatest interest to
trade visitors.

> **Promontobor**
> 3909 Mád, Kölcsey utca 10
> T: +36 47 348 000

TÁLLYA

THIS PLEASANT little village, ten kilometres along Road 38 going north from Disznókő and 20 kilometres from Tokaj, has an interesting claim to fame. It is the geometric centre of Europe and boasts a three-metre-high wooden carving of a stork to mark the spot.

MIHÁLY HOLLÓKŐI

THE HOLLÓKŐI FAMILY has been involved in winemaking for generations and has ten prime hectares in the Tállya region, produc-

> **Mihály Hollókői**
> 3907 Tállya, Bocskai utca 10
> T: +36 47 398 028

ing a range of wines in the deep cellars underneath the popular restaurant that attracts more diners than any other in the Tokaji region. So many English-speaking visitors come to the restaurant that the labels on the washroom doors read 'Ladies' and 'Gents'.

APART FROM THE NOVELTY of being at the geometrical centre of Europe, the alfresco dining area offers splendid views of the surrounding wine country from its vine-covered terrace.

THE LARGE AND VARIED menu includes many regional specialities, and the friendly atmosphere is conducive to good conversation accompanied by Hollókői's well-made wines. Visitors who go in June can pluck ripe cherries from the trees in the garden.

LÁSZLÓ WINERY

GYULA LÁSZLÓ originated from Transylvania but emigrated to South Africa, where he was instrumental in shaping their wine exports for European markets before coming to Tokaj.

LÁSZLÓ AND HIS PARTNERS have 25 hectares but have plans to

László Winery
3907 Tállya, Dobogó utca 47
T: +36 47 398 182
3907 Tállya, Bocskai utca 10
T: +36 47 398 028
Directions: Continue through Tállya past the wooden stork marking the geometric centre of Europe and you will find the winery in a tall old millhouse on your left.

extend the size of their estate to 100 hectares, which would make it the largest winery in the Mád Basin after Royal Tokaj. The focus is on the three classic grapes of the region – Furmint, Hárslevelű and Yellow Muscat – but there is also growing interest in Kövérszőlő.

THE WINERY IS WELL-EQUIPPED with all the latest technology required to make sound, reductive wines. The old cellars are well-stocked with maturing late-harvest and Aszú wines.

ABAÚJSZÁNTÓ

THE OLD CELLAR row at Abaújszántó houses several small wineries, among which we recommend Pendits for a visit. The drive up the Hernád Valley towards the Slovakian border makes a very pleasant day out.

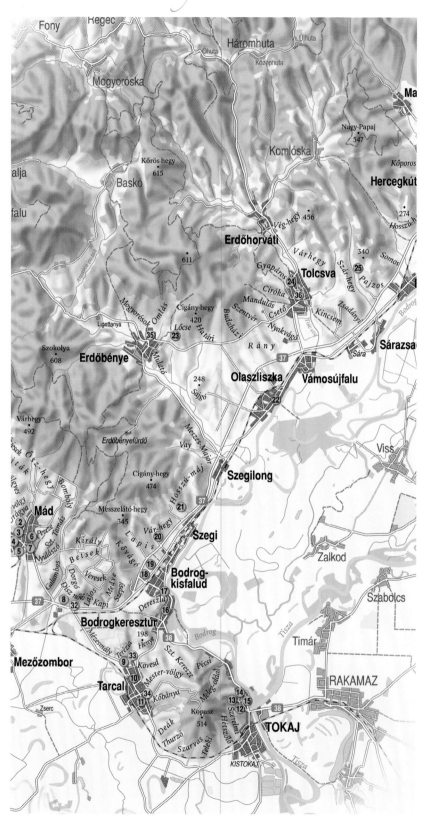

Erdőbénye and Tolcsva

ERDŐBÉNYE, one of the oldest settlements in the Zemplén Foothills, is an extremely pleasant and peaceful place to stay, close to a conservation area. The proximity to the Zemplén forests makes it an ideal home for one of the leading Tokaji cooperages.

ACCOMMODATIONS IN ERDŐBÉNYE

HOTEL MAGITA

The newly-built Hotel Magita in the centre of Erdőbénye has 24 bright and airy bedrooms, an excellent restaurant, and its own leisure facilities – including a ten-pin bowling alley.

The hotel owes its name to an intelligent and beautiful young woman who lived in Erdőbénye during the Turkish invasion of the region around 1550. The family house became a refuge for settlers fleeing the Turks, and when they eventually attacked the house two young Turkish officers fell in love with Magita, the daughter of the house, who was already betrothed.

Hotel Magita
3932 Erdőbénye, Mátyás Király utca 49
T: +36 47 536 400
F: +36 47 536 401
magitahotel@freemail.hu,
info@hotel-magita.hu
www.hotel-magita.hu

She devised a successful scheme to capture the Turks, but they broke out and threatened to burn down the house. Another Turkish soldier (who had also fallen in love with Magita) helped her escape, but she drowned in the attempt. The Turkish invaders were so desolate at her death that they left Erdőbénye forever. However, the people of Erdőbénye have not forgotten her beauty and kindness to her fellow citizens, hence the hotel name.

DINING IN ERDŐBÉNYE AND TOLCSVA

MAGITA RESTAURANT

One glance at the menu leaves you doubtless that you are in a winemaking community also renowned for its cooperages. The first item on the expansive menu is a potato soup with mangalica sausage, the traditional lunch of vineyard

> **Magita Restaurant**
> 3932 Erdőbénye, Mátyás Király utca 49
> T: +36 47 536 406

workers; the second is a knuckle stew, the delight of cellar men; while a third is the pork-chop dish preferred by the coopers. All three dishes are made with Tokaji wine.

The restaurant also caters for mere mortals enjoying cuisine that makes use of local wines. Hare is jugged in Furmint, baked fogas fish is served with a Tokaj wine sauce, and roast duck is offered with grilled pears basted in honey and braised in Tokaj wine. There is also the prospect of game and red-meat dishes prepared to accompany fine Aszú wines.

ŐS KAJÁN

Do not look for a grandiose building, just a slightly larger-than-normal traditional farm-house (with a car park) from which a restaurant has been brilliantly adapted, spreading over several rooms.

Owners Pascal Leeman and Anne Roy have drawn on the rich food resources of the region to create a cuisine that includes many fresh, homegrown ingredients, served with a handpicked selection of Tokaji wines.

"We believe that it is important to reflect the village atmosphere," says Leeman, "because the ingredients for our cuisine come from the countryside around us. We grow 15 types of aromatic herbs and spices in our garden, many of our own vegetables and edible flowers, and we purchase others locally."

While many diners may consider the predominantly sweet wines of Tokaj as dessert wines, Leeman asserts that the wine's culinary potential is much wider. "Ős Kaján is a workshop. Drawing our inspiration from old Hungarian and bourgeois cuisine we have found that Tokaji Aszú 6-puttonyos goes extremely well with duck and deer, especially in sauces," he says. "Wines are part of our work as well as our hobby."

Design and entertainment are also an integral part of the Ős Kaján experience.

In each of the dining rooms, different artistic compositions reflect different moods, and from time to time Ős Kaján hosts contemporary art exhibitions. In the summer months the restaurant puts on musical concerts in its garden, or entertainments such as readings given by writer Péter Esterházy from his own work, alternating with jazz compositions from László Dés. Check the Ős Kaján website for special events prior to your visit.

Ős Kaján

3934 Tolcsva, Kossuth utca 14-16
T & F: +36 47 384 195
oskajan.restaurant@axelero.hu
www.oskajan.hu

Directions: From Tokaj and Sarospatak take Road 37 before turning off to Tolcsva. As you drive into Tolcsva you will see signposts to Oremus Winery on your left. Continue on the road for another 100 metres or so and turn right at the T junction. Ős Kaján is 100 metres on your left. From Erdőbénye, Ős Kaján is seven kilometers. The minor road joins the main road on the outskirts of the town and you will soon see the signpost for Oremus. Continue as above.

WINERIES

BÉRES

DR. JÓZSEF BÉRES was born to the founder of Hungary's famous Béres herbal remedies. His late father would be proud of his son's investment in this fine new winery at Erdőbénye, one of the region's oldest settlements amid its pre-eminent winemaking communities. Dr. Béres believes that Tokaj is a national treasure and that Hungarians have a duty to take good care of it and its wines.

THUS A GREAT DEAL of thought went into the design and construction of the new winery, housing state-of-the-art winemaking equipment and facilities to handle the production from 45 hectares of vines from 2008.

THE WINERY has also been planned to accommodate the growing number of wine tourists. Locally quarried white and yellow limestone and Zemplén oak from the nearby forests have been used imaginatively in the overall construction, and we admired the many thoughtful touches in the decoration and furnishing of the splendid visitor-reception facilities.

HOWEVER, the building would mean little without the production of wines that reflect the nature of this special terroir. The pride

Béres
3932 Erdőbénye,
Vörösmarty utca 6
T: +36 47 536 000
F: +36 47 536 001
info@beresbor.hu
www.beresbor.hu
Directions: From Tokaj travel through Bodrogkeresztúr to Road 37, then take the left turn signposted to Erdőbénye. Follow the signs to Béres, a modern winery on the eastern outskirts of the town.
Owner: Béres Family
Estate: 90ha, 45ha under vine planted at a density of 5,570 vines per hectare on a low cordon.
Varieties planted: Furmint 50%, Hárslevelű 30%, Yellow Muscat 12%, Zéta 4%, Kövérszőlő 4%
Tour and tasting cost: From Ft 2,500
Visiting hours: By appointment 10:00-16:00
Languages spoken: English, German

and joy of the winery is the ten-hectare Lőcse Vineyard, along with a further 35 hectares in the superbly located Omlás, Diókút, and Barkóczi vineyards.

THE APPOINTMENT OF SAROLTA BÁRDOS as Chief Winemaker was a key factor in the development of the estate's wines. Her debut wine was a stunning barrel-fermented 2003 Dry Furmint, made from the Lőcse's wonderfully ripe grapes and matured in small oak barrels, conferring a rich creamy flavour on the fruity wine.

THE 2003 LATE-HARVEST LŐCSE was equally impressive. The linden-flower and honeyed aroma was enhanced by the Furmint's fine acids, resulting in a wine with wonderful balance and purity of taste.

THE WINEMAKER acknowledged her luck in starting with a good vintage, but Bárdos's confident touch is evident in the 2005 and 2006 vintages now available, and in her handling of oak that gives her wines extra flavour. Being a young mother, Bárdos recently resigned and was replaced by Péter Hudák, another talented winemaker.

ERDŐBÉNYE APPEARS TO HAVE overtaken Gönc as the barrel-making centre of Tokaji, and its coopers are as keen to familiarise themselves with modern winemaking styles as winemakers are keen to best use the particular properties of Zemplén oak.

BÉRES IS A VERY ATTRACTIVE winery to visit not only because it is new and well-designed, but also because its wines are both stylish and exciting. We expect it to become one of the leading wineries of the region.

Range of Wines

DRY FURMINT 2005 The follow-up to the brilliant 2003 wine. Elegant, well-structured wine with mellow acids, and benefiting from careful oak treatment.

HÁRSLEVELŰ 2005 A dry version of this variety which is more often seen in semisweet or late-harvest style. Crisp with a mineral character, and good fruity flavour.

YELLOW MUSCAT 2005 A tropical-fruit aroma and lovely fresh acids make it a joy to drink as an aperitif or just as a conversation wine.

LATE-HARVEST HÁRSLEVELŰ 2005 CLASSIC SELECTION Intense fruit flavours from lovely ripe grapes. Full-bodied and a fine example of this variety and style.

TOKAJI CUVEE 2004 The Furmint and Hárslevelű were harvested and vinified together, producing a highly concentrated wine of 150g/l sugar.

LŐCSE VINEYARD

The vineyard has a south-southwesterly aspect and is well-protected from cold northerly and easterly winds. The rhyolite tuff soil, containing minerals like zeolite and quartz, warms up quickly and grapes ripen prodigiously in this favourable microclimate.

The Lőcse slope, inclined at an angle of 35 degrees, drains well. Furmint and Hárslevelű dominate the plantings, but there is also Yellow Muscat, Zéta, and Kövérszőlő.

The first Béres wines from the vineyard in 2003 reveal the site's enormous potential. As the young plantation matures the wines will surely develop further and become even more giving. This one of the most interesting vineyards we visited because of its soil, microclimate and inclination.

VIVAMUS

HUNGARIAN AND SPANISH interests combined to purchase and rebuild this winery and its extensive 3.5-kilometre cellar network extending under the Reform Church in Erdőbénye. The old cellar entrance was on the front side of the Reform Church.

LIKE SO MANY OTHERS in the region the cellars, once used by the Rákóczis, are on two levels and go to a depth of 18 metres. Vivamus's 26 hectares of vineyard are stretched out between Szegilong and Tolcsva, and like their near neighbour Babits, the higher reaches of the vineyards afford spellbinding autumnal views of the Bodrog water meadows.

THE AVERAGE VINTAGE starts on 25th October and continues into mid-November, with one hectare left unharvested in hope that ice-wine can be made. The 2006 Jegnectar has 190g/l residual sugar and wonderful honey flavours.

Vivamus
3932 Erdőbénye, Ady köz 1
T: +36 47 536 014
borkereskedelem@vivamus.hu
www.vivamus.hu
Directions: From Tokaj take Road 38 and then right on Road 37, follow the signs into Erdőbénye and head for the Reform Church. Ady köz runs alongside and you will find the new cellar entrance at No. 1.

1995 WAS A GOOD VINTAGE for sweet and dry Szamorodni wines. The Dry Szamorodni turned out to be a magnificent libation. It was five years in wood where it developed complex flavours

under a thin film of flor, and is still in excellent condition. It is one of the finest dry Szamorodni wines that we tasted.

AS ELSEWHERE in Tokaj the real test of a house is on the quality of their Aszú, and Vivamus was delighted to win the Gold Medal for best Hungarian wine at the 2005 Tokyo International Wine Competition, judged by some of the world's most experienced wine experts. Apart from Japan, Vivamus sells well in the USA and Belgium.

ZOLTÁN OLÁH runs the winery with his wife and daughter. His father was a director of the defunct Borkombinát, but Oláh is pleased that those days of attempting to make good wine under near-impossible conditions are well and truly behind.

HOMONNA

ATTILA HOMONNA's slight frame masks his strength and determination to make excellent wine. A young man with a mission, he set out from Erdőbénye with his backpack and guitar, and for three peripatetic years worked his way up through European vineyards, often making wine in five different regions each year. His somewhat laid-back style and hippie-like appearance seems at odds with his absolute devotion to his vineyards and his winemaking.

HOMONNA'S HARD WORK and persistence paid off when he acquired a few precious hectares in the Határi Vineyard on the superb south-facing slopes above Erdőbénye, and at Meszesmajor.

Homonna
3932 Erdőbénye, Hunyadi utca 61
T: +36 47 336 082
homonna@homonna.com
www.homonna.com
Directions: Hunyadi is a small street running off Mátyás Király utca.

THE VERY OLD STAKE-PLANTED VINES in Határi produced the 2005 off-dry Furmint, and a late-harvested Furmint with 87g/l residual sugar that were both widely admired. He has high hopes for its 2006 successor.

WE ARE CONFIDENT THAT this hardworking young vintner will produce many more fine wines, both for his own company and Obsidian, a new company formed by Péter Kovács, who also has an excellent plot in Határi.

KARÁDI ÉS BERGER

A START-UP WITH a five-hectare estate in good vineyards like Vay, along with a heavy leaning towards Furmint, which accounts for 80% of their plantings. The

> **Karádi és Berger**
> 3932 Erdőbénye, Hunyadi utca 38
> T: +36 20 927 4665 (mobile)
> boraszat@karadiesberger.hu
> www.karadiesberger.hu

sweet Szamorodni that we tasted showed style and promise and we look forward to sampling further wines from this fledgling winery.

PATRICIUS

THIS ATTRACTIVE new winery is an act of faith in the future of Tokaj as a pre-eminent wine-producing region. The Kékessy Family believes, as did their ancestors, that Tokaj has a unique terroir and that it is an honour to be associated with it.

THE FAMILY APPOINTED Dr. Péter Molnár as General Manager in 2001 and he oversaw the development of the vineyards and new winery, as well as the range of wines produced.

THE 80 HECTARES of First Growth vineyards are in eight different locations ranging from the loess of Tokaj Hill to the clay soils of the Mád Basin and the nyirok soils around Bodrogkisfalud. The Lapis and Várhegy vineyards can be seen from the winery veranda.

MOLNÁR'S DISCIPLINED APPROACH to viticultural practice is in keeping with his record as a teaching academic. He knows the importance of producing top-quality fruit and is restless in his search for the best. During his time at the Tarcal Research Centre he worked on the development of Kövérszőlő and clearly has a bond with this grape. But he is also keen to test older varieties and clones, and has planted a selection in front of the winery so that he can keep an eye on them.

HOWEVER, LIKE OTHER GREAT TOKAJI vintners he believes Furmint is a real treasure; a Pontian variety that has really taken to the volcanic soils of the region. The winery's Dry Furmint reveals his sure handling of the variety,

and the award-winning single-vineyard Aszú 6-puttonyos Bendecz shows superb balance thanks to the very fine acids that Furmint delivers.

MOLNÁR IS VERY PARTICULAR ABOUT WOOD; he insists that there is more to the issue than choosing the right type of oak for each wine. Once he settles on the source of his oak he looks for staves that have been properly dried out over three or four summers, and for coopers that show sensitivity to the special needs of the Patricius wines.

Patricius

3917 Bodrogkisfalud
T: +36 47 396 001
F: +36 47 596 027
info@patricius.hu
www.patricius.hu
Directions: From Tokaj take Road 38 through Bodrogkeresztúr, turning right on to Road 37 towards Sarospatak. Patricius Winery is clearly signposted at milepost 41-42.
Owners: Kékessy Family
Estate: 80ha under vine planted at a density of 5,700 vines per hectare on a low cordon.
Varieties planted: Furmint 63%, Hárslevelű 17%, Yellow Muscat 10%, Zéta 10%
Visiting hours: 9:00-15:00 by appointment
Tour and tasting cost: From Ft 1,500
Languages spoken: English

THIS IS AN IMPRESSIVE new winery enthusiastically managed by a gifted winemaker, and we expect it to establish a position in the top flight of Tokaji wineries.

Range of Wines

DRY FURMINT 2005 Made from very healthy ripe grapes, mostly fermented in stainless steel. However, 25% is barrel-fermented, providing extra body and flavour that make this such an outstanding wine.

ASZÚ 5-PUTTONYOS 2000 Lovely apricot and peach flavours with sugar and acids in balance, and a mineral background that will sustain the wine well over the next decade or so.

ASZÚ 6-PUTTONYOS 2000 BENDECZ
A very classy single-vineyard wine with intense apricot and raisin aromas, elegant acids, and a fine creamy finish. We admired the restraint, the lack of flamboyance, and the concentration on sound structure and balance.

BENDECZ VINEYARD

The deep rhyolite tuff is planted with 70% Furmint and 30% Hárslevelű. One of the advantages of this soil is that it breaks up easily, allowing the roots to push deep into the base rock, which provides the nutrients that will keep the wine fresh throughout its life and gives it the rich mineral character that distinguishes Tokaji wines.
The vineyard is on a steep south-southwest-facing slope near a huge stone quarry, and enjoys a special microclimate. The soil and elements combine to produce a wine with a delightful floral bouquet, good length on the palate, smooth elegance, and strong personality. The 2000 Aszú 6-Puttonyos was a Champion Wine and drew much-deserved praise to the winery and its team of vintners.

HUNGAROVIN

THE WINERY IS NOT OPEN to members of the public, but trade visits can be made by appointment through Törley at their Budapest telephone number or e-mail address. Do not forget to ask for directions as the winery is off the beaten track.

THE PRIZED 43.5 HECTARES in the south-facing Kővágó Vineyard belong to Hungarovin, the Törley subsidiary responsible for the company's expanding Tokaj business.

KŐVÁGÓ MEANS 'stonecutter' or 'quarryman', and gives a strong clue as to the nature of the soil in the vineyard. Actually, it is clay mixed with broken stone in which Furmint and Hárslevelű thrive, yielding wines of great character and finesse.

Hungarovin
3916 Bodrogkeresztúr
T: +36 1 424 2500 (Törley)
info@hungarovin.hu
www.hungarovin.hu

THE LIBATIONS ARE made by the vastly experienced and amiable winemaker János Puklus, and sold under the St. Stephan's Crown label. St. Stephan was the first King of Hungary, whose coronation was blessed by Pope Sylvester II, who sent the new king a magnificent crown. The same crown, after many adventures in its thousand-year history, can now be seen in the House of Parliament in Budapest. It is one of Hungary's most precious treasures.

ALL THE ST. STEPHAN'S CROWN TOKAJI ASZÚ WINES, and the superb Dry Szamorodni, are aged for longer than usual before being released. They are well-distributed throughout Hungary, in key European markets, and in Japan. In our opinion these wines, made in the traditional style by modern vintners, offer excellent value for money. The 1998 Aszú Eszencia makes a wonderful Father's Day gift.

Range of Wines

ST. STEPHAN'S CROWN TOKAJ FURMINT 2006 Light-green colour with well-defined ripe peach aromas and flavours supported by keen acids. An elegant and enjoyable wine.

ST. STEPHAN'S CROWN SWEET SZAMORODNI 1999 A lovely medium-deep golden colour with apricot, peach, and melon flavours. A soft palate and long pleasant aftertaste make this a very attractive aperitif.

ST. STEPHAN'S CROWN 3-PUTTONYOS ASZÚ 1999 Light-golden colour and intense apricot aromas with well-integrated acids. An elegant and charming wine.

ST. STEPHAN'S CROWN 5-PUTTONYOS ASZÚ 1999 Light-golden colour with complex aromas of honey, honeysuckle, and marmalade. The crisp acids lift the palate and give a smooth creamy finish. An accomplished and fine wine.

ST. STEPHAN'S CROWN ASZÚ ESZENCIA 1988 Almost mahogany in colour, it has overripe plum and raisin aromas, with marvellous sugar concentration nicely balanced with elegant acids and a long, satisfying finish.

ST. STEPHAN'S CROWN DRY SZAMORODNI 1983 Medium-gold in colour, enticing dried-fruit aromas, bone-dry, refined and elegant. A superb example of this style increasingly admired by gourmets.

CROWN ESTATES

CROWN ESTATES WAS formed in 1993 from the rump of the Borkombinát, the all-powerful trading house of the communist period. The company inherited two highly prized assets: 40 hectares of the Great Growth Szarvas Vineyard, together with a further 40 hectares in First Growth vineyards around Mád and Tolcsva, and also the Museum Collection of old Aszú wines – including a few old bottles of vintages between 1642 and the 1890s – and commercial quantities of all celebrated 20th-century vintages from 1900.

THERE IS NO OTHER CELLAR that we know of with so many rare and eminently drinkable vintages. James Halliday, the famous Australian winemaker and a colleague in the Circle of Wine Writers, remembers tasting a 1642 Aszú which had dried up somewhat but was still clean and drinkable. Michael Broadbent MW, Director of Christie's Auction House in London, who has probably tasted more old vintages of Tokaj than any other non-Hungarian wine taster, confirms in his book *Vintage Wine* that the magnificent Comet vintage of 1811 was in excellent condition when he tasted it three decades ago.

IN SEPTEMBER 2000, the Hungarian State presented the late HM Queen Mother with a bottle of 1900 Aszú 6-Puttonyos to mark her 100th birthday. The chief winemaker provided the following notes on the wine, that was aged in the traditional 136-litre gönci cask for 12 years before bottling.

Crown Estates

3980 Sátoraljaújhely, Mártírok utca 17
T: +36 47 322 133
F: +36 47 322 816
tokajvin@mail.matav.hu
www.crownestates-tokaji.com
Directions: The cathedral-like vaulted cellars at Szegi are on Road 37 about 12km from Tokaj through Bodrogkeresztúr, or 10km past Disznókő. The cellars are clearly visible from the road. The Szarvas Vineyard is located almost halfway between Tarcal and Tokaj on the slopes of Tokaj Hill. There are tracks leading to the old field research building.
Owner: The Republic of Hungary
Estate: 80ha under vine. New plantings have been made at a density of 5,000 vines per hectare on a medium cordon on 40ha of Szarvas (Tarcal), and in Király (Mád) and Szentvér (Tolcsva)
Varieties planted: Furmint 70%, Hárslevelű 25%, Yellow Muscat and Kövérszőlő 5%
Tour and tasting cost: From Ft 2,000
Visiting times: By appointment
Languages spoken: English

Colour:	*Dark amber but still looking young.*
Aroma:	*Old furniture and spice.*
Palate:	*Fine sugar component and tight fresh acidity.*
Finish:	*Elegant and long. A wine of poise and distinction.*

THE 15TH-CENTURY CELLARS provide ideal conditions for the maturation of such great wines. They hold the temperature stable between 10-12°C and retain 90% humidity. The longevity of the great Aszú wines speaks for the very special nature of the Tokaji terroirs.

CROWN ESTATES has recently appointed Gergő Szendei as Chief Winemaker. There has been a vast improvement in the quality of the varietal wines made under the Crown Estates Castle Island label, and with the first Aszú wines from the new plantings in the Szarvas Vineyard about to be released, the company is well-poised to build its international sales.

THE CASTLE ISLAND NAME derives from the 15th-century Tokaj Castle, built on a small island at the confluence of the Bodrog and Tisza rivers. The island fortress was of such great strategic importance that it was destroyed by the Transylvanians themselves during the Hungarian War of Independence (1703-1711), for fear that it may be taken by the enemy. However, its name lives on in a range of wines that reflects all that is best in contemporary Tokaj; healthy grapes extremely well-vinified with the trademark mineral character of Tokaji.

CROWN ESTATES ASZÚS HAVE also regained their former lustre. The single-vineyard Great Growth Szarvas wines of 1993, 1994 and 1996 are still available from the company, and we look forward with anticipation to the release of the 1999, 2000 and 2002 vintages. These great wines help us understand why libations from the Szarvas Vineyard were designated "fit for the king's table."

Range of Wines

CASTLE ISLAND DRY FURMINT 2006 Fresh, crisp and nicely balanced and full of flavour. Superb value for money.

CASTLE ISLAND LATE-HARVEST FURMINT 2006 Well-ripened grapes that show the Furmint at its most flavoursome. A wonderful summer-afternoon conversation wine. A perfect excuse to indulge in almond-flavoured patisserie!

CASTLE ISLAND LATE-HARVEST HÁRSLEVELŰ 2006 Another well-made wine with an appealing linden-flower nose and honey flavour that represents the variety at its best.

CASTLE ISLAND LATE-HARVEST YELLOW MUSCAT 2006 The Muscat aromas are really enchanting. The sugar/acid balance is well-handled and makes this is a very satisfying wine.

CROWN ESTATE ASZÚ 6-PUTTONYOS 2002 A bold wine with an assertive character. We liked the harmony that comes with the superb selection of grapes from three quite different First Growth vineyards – a polished and refined example of the traditional style.

SZARVAS SINGLE-VINEYARD ASZÚ 4-PUTTONYOS 1994 For many vintners the 1994 Aszús posed problems due to poor weather. The Szarvas Vineyard proved its class by yielding grapes good enough to make top-quality wines. This 4-puttonyos has an extraordinary copper-red colour, an assortment of aromas, and an agreeable nutty, raisiny taste that is developing well. This is a classy wine from a great vineyard.

SZARVAS VINEYARD

Szarvas, named as one of the two Great Growths in the classification of 1737, lies on south-facing slopes of Tokaj Hill between Tarcal and Tokaj town. It owes prominence to its superb location at about 130-200 metres above the confluence of the Tisza and Bodrog, where the flood plain is most expansive and botrytisation is most effective.

In 1867 Szarvas was given the title of Imperial and Royal Court Vineyard, and it continued to supply the Habsburg Dynasty until Hungary became a Republic in 1918.

Furmint is the dominant variety in the vineyard, along with 25% Hárslevelű, and 5% Yellow Muscat and Kövérszőlő planted on a medium cordon. The loess soil retains the heat of the sun and ensures a high level of ripeness that adds extra richness to the wines. Vinicultural practices such as disbudding and cluster-thinning ensure that the healthiest grapes prosper. Szarvas single-vineyard Aszú wines are still made in the traditional manner, with long, slow ageing in wood. They are made in a style that is still widely appreciated in Hungary but not so well-understood elsewhere. During the maturation period the barrels are not topped up after fermentation and a thin flor develops on the wine, contributing to its richness of flavour and complexity. This longer, slower maturation means that Szarvas 6-puttonyos Aszús are not normally released until eight or nine years after the vintage.

DUSÓCZKY

TAMÁS DUSÓCZKY is one of the great characters of Tokaj. Scion of an aristocratic family that lost all its land in the communist period, he immigrated to Switzerland where he pursued a brilliant career in the computer industry. On retirement at the age of 65 he returned to Hungary to renew his love affair with Tokaj.

HE ACQUIRED six hectares in the Hosszú-Mály Vineyard near Szegi, rebuilt the old family winery and renovated the family's traditional farmhouse. Despite the long years of separation with Tokaj, Dusóczky was determined to play his part in the revival of its Aszú wines, and asked the experienced vintner László Kubus to help him. Dusóczky wines have the dark golden colour and rich opulent flavours associated with traditional Aszús; they are just the wines to share over a good conversation and a fine Havana cigar.

AT THE 2007 BUDAPEST WINE FESTIVAL, Dusóczky offered us slices of a wonderfully nutty chocolate cake specially made for him by Joseph Auguste, son of a family famous for its pastries since the 1850s. He also told us about his family's connection with the Mariassys, the oldest known landowners in Tokaji, who later married into the aristocratic Waldbott Family in the 19th century.

BY FAR THE MOST INTERESTING news he imparted was about the Aszú wines from the 1600s purchased and cellared by Warsaw's famous Fukier wine merchants. Commandeered by Hitler, they were carried off to Berlin. Fortunately, Hitler did not take to them and they ended up in safe storage at Yalta. After WWII they were taken over by the Russians, and Marshall Zhukov brought them back to Berlin.

> **Dusóczky**
> 3918 Szegi, Dusóczky Tanya 1
> T & F: +36 47 309 058
> dusoczky@axelero.hu
> www.tokaj-wines.com

CELLAR VISITS ARE by appointment only, though English and German is spoken. Dusóczky wines are available for tasting and purchase at the House of Hungarian Wines on Castle Hill in Budapest.

VAY

> **Vay**
> Budapest 1026, Trombitás u. 13a
> T: +36 1 214 9627

WE HAVE INCLUDED this small winery owned by the esteemed historian Krisztián Ungváry, who resides in Budapest, because of the quality of the wines he produces from two hectares in the vineyard near Szegilong named after Baron Miklós Vay. Baron Vay was largely responsible for introducing the now-well-established specially shaped 50cl Tokaji wine bottle, because he believed that "the English will buy more Aszú in bottle than in the cask."

Krisztián Ungváry openly admits his admiration of the Furmint that provides the structure for his two wines – a late-harvest Furmint and a Cuvee. The 2005 vintage of the Cuvee was beautifully balanced. Ripe grapes gave a wine rich in residual sugar with fine acids. Ungváry can be contacted at his Budapest number, and his wines are available through Bortársaság (T: +36 1 212 2569).

SAMUEL TINON

Samuel Tinon is a young winemaker with a unique story. He is a Frenchman born in the sweet-wine producing area of St. Croix du Mont, who fell in love with Tokaj and brought his young family to the region to establish a winery in Olaszliszka.

He is also different in that he brings a particular and very precise approach to his winemaking, and is inclined to follow his nose in developing wines such as his 2001 Dry Szamorodni. Tinon believes that Dry Szamorodni is the best expression of Furmint. He admits to learning a great deal about vine-

Samuel Tinon
3933 Olaszliszka, Bánom utca 8
T: +36 47 358 405
samueltinon@samueltinon.com
www.samueltinon.com
Directions: From Tokaj take Road 38 through Bodrogkeresztur, turning right onto Road 37. After a few kilometres turn right towards Olaszliszka and follow the road into the village. Tinon is on the left just before the church.
Visiting hours: By appointment only.
Languages spoken: English, French, Spanish, and Italian

yard and cellar work during his 16 years in Tokaj, and his wines show him to be a winemaker worth following.

He first came to work at Royal Tokaj in 1991 when István Szepsy was vintner, and stayed in Mád for three years before travelling the world as a flying winemaker. He returned to Tokaj to work with András Bacsó at Oremus from 1996-99, and started his own winery in 2000.

Tinon established his pedigree with his first wines – an Aszú 5-puttonyos and

Aszú-Eszencia from the 2000 vintage. Both wines have the hallmark of class and are selling well in Paris, Tokyo, New York and London. However, his most intriguing wine is the 2001 Dry Szamorodni, stimulated by his experience working in Jerez and developed by his knowledge of Vin Jaune d'Arbois.

"DRY SZAMORODNI may not be the most glamorous of models on the catwalk," Tinon explains, "but it is like a woman with genuine character and poise in whose company most intelligent men would rather be."

THE QUALITY OF TINON'S WINES has led to a steady growth in sales. He works hard at his craft and has just completed a cellar extension. He welcomes visitors by appointment, and does not charge a sampling fee but is always grateful when visitors purchase a bottle or two. His range is limited by design and includes an excellent sweet Szamorodni and a very agreeable dry wine simply labelled Tino Dry. Later this year Tinon plans to establish an international Tokaj Appreciation Society and will be actively recruiting members from those that visit him in Tokaj.

OREMUS

OREMUS, THE LATIN WORD FOR 'LET US PRAY', was the first word used in official documents of the 16th century when Transylvania was the first country in the world to practice religious tolerance.

IT IS ALSO THE NAME of the vineyard from which Chaplain Laczkó Szepsi harvested the botrytised grapes to make an Aszú wine for Zsuzsanna Lorántffy, the wife of ruling Prince György Rákóczi I. Later, the grape variety was named Oremus. However, in 1994 it was changed to Zéta to avoid confusion with the newly created Oremus Estate.

OREMUS IS ONE of the most handsome wineries in Hungary. The winery building's stylish architecture complements the landscaped parkland above the small town of Tolcsva, surrounded by the vine-clad Zemplén Hills.

THE ESTATE IS OWNED by the Alvarez Family, proprietors of Vega Sicilia in Ribera del Duero, one of Spain's premier wineries. The family recognises Tokaj as one of the world's most blessed wine regions and wanted to invest in its renaissance.

ANDRÁS BACSÓ leads Oremus as General Manager, applying his genuine passion for making Tokaji wines through his knowledge of the terroirs, grape varieties and Tokaji traditions. He is also alive to the possibilities of modern technology, in sync with the owner's desire to make classical Tokaji wines using up-to-date equipment.

OREMUS IS NOT homogeneous like other estates sold off in the first round of privatisation. Disznókő, Hétszőlő, Pajzos and Megyer had long-since been known as single-vineyard estates. Bacsó recommended that the Oremus vineyard holding be spread across different Tokaji terroirs because they would give him varied flavours of wines.

THE CORE OF THE HOLDING is in clay/nyirok soils that make up the hills around Tolcsva. Their other strategic sites are in the loess soils of Tokaj Hill and the clay soils of the Mád Basin, while the famous Oremus Vineyard on Sátor Hill has fine-grained mineral soil. All the selected vineyard plots are in First Growths where vines are pruned back to eight bunches per vine.

OREMUS HAS a slightly different varietal policy to other wineries. Whereas Furmint and Hárslevelű dominate, Zéta contributes rather more than at other wineries – not only because the variety was once called Oremus, but also because the Furmint/Bouvier cross ripens early, botrytises well, and is considered a useful insurance policy against excessive rain or cold.

Oremus

3934 Tolcsva, Bajcsy-
Zsilinszky utca 45
T: +36 47 384 505
F: +36 47 384 504
oremus93@t-online.hu
www.tokajoremus.com
Directions: Take Road
38 through
Bodrogkeresztúr, turn
right onto Road 37, and
continue to the signs for
Tolcsva. Follow the signs
to the winery.
Owner: Vega Sicilia SA
Estate: 115ha, with
100ha under vine, most-
ly planted at 5,700 vines
per hectare on a low
cordon in new planta-
tions. Oremus jealously
guards healthy, old,
stake-planted vines.
Varieties planted:
Furmint 44%, Hárslevelű
18%, Zéta 18%, Yellow
Muscat 10%
Tour and tasting cost:
From Ft 2,000
Languages spoken:
English, French,
Spanish, and Italian

BACSÓ IS A VERY thorough vintner. He app-
roaches every stage of the winemaking process
with great care and attention, continually testing
grape sugar must and acidity levels to ensure
grape harvesting at the optimum moment, while
ruthlessly discarding any damaged or unfit
grapes. His gravity-fed production line keeps
grapes from being pumped and pushed about,
thus avoiding problems of stabilization, clarifica-
tion, and oxidation which require chemical treatments to correct.

MACERATION of the aszú berries with the base
wine takes place in large, slowly turning steel
drums. The must is then gently pressed before
the precious liquid is filled into new oak for fermentation and maturation.

THE CUVEE IS MADE in a similar painstaking
way. Ripe grapes (some botrytised, some not),
are vinified in bunches. Fermentation is quite rapid and stopped when
the desired level of residual sugar has been achieved. The wine is then
filled into new oak and matured for six months before bottling and a further period of ageing. The net result is a fresher wine, bursting with fresh
fruit flavours.

APART FROM ITS GREAT ASZÚ and Cuvee wines, Oremus produces an excellent dry Furmint named Mandolás. The wine is barrel-fermented, left on
its lees, and aged for 12 months after bottling.

NEW WOOD PLAYS an important part in the making of Oremus wines. The
winery buys and matures its own Zemplén oak, which is made into barrels
by local coopers under contract. The winery uses around 5,000 barrels each
year for the new harvest.

LIKE ALL TOP WINERIES, Oremus constantly seeks to improve its viticulture
and vinification methods. Currently tests are underway to assess the suit-
ability of pre-phylloxera grape varieties, experiments are being carried out
on different types of oak, and new techniques for improving the base wine
are being developed.

THIS IS AN EXCELLENT WINERY to visit because every stage of production can be easily seen and explained. Here, one can handle samples of the different rocks forming the geological basis of the Tokaji region, inspect winemaking utensils, and look at detailed wine maps of the region.

Range of Wines

MANDOLÁS DRY FURMINT 2005
Lovely golden colour with a vivid bouquet. Peach and almond flavours. Superb balance and long aftertaste. An excellent wine widely distributed.

ASZÚ 5-PUTTONYOS 2000 Pale golden colour. Rich aromas from Zéta, Muscat, and Hárslevelű; fine acids from Furmint. This is an outstanding wine and shows the newcomer to Tokaj just what heights can be achieved.

ASZÚ 6-PUTTONYOS 1999 An outstanding wine. Pale-honey colour, gentle but satisfying aromas. The vintage produced wonderfully ripe fruit, and confident, polished winemaking has translated it into a rich carnival of flavours lingering in the mouth for some time.

PANNON TOKAJ

PANNON IS A MIDSIZED venture started in 2000 to produce value-for-money wines for the mass market, as well as some finer Aszús sold under its Dominium label. Of the 25 hectares harvested, nine are old Furmint while another six are Yellow Muscat, a variety which does extremely well in the clay soils around Tolcsva.

VINTNER ATTILA KIRMIN was assistant winemaker at Dégenfeld, and is used to making fresh and fruity reductive wines that are liked locally. The Aszú wines are made from selected berries and barrel-aged for a maximum of two years to keep them young and fresh. The Aszú 6-Puttonyos 2001 was particularly successful, and the 2003 Late-Harvest Furmint is showing exotic fruit flavours supported by firm acids.

PANNON IS NOT YET prepared for unannounced visits, but is happy to receive guests who book in advance. Wines can be tasted by appointment at their Budapest offices at Daróczi út 1-3.

Pannon Tokaj
3934 Tolcsva, Arany utca 14
T: +36 47 584 056
info@pannontokaj.hu
www.pannontokaj.hu
Directions: As for Oremus, but look for Arany János utca before you get to Oremus.

TOLCSVA BOR

THE SAJGÓ FAMILY WINERY owns 15 hectares passed from father to son whenever political circumstances allowed. The Sajgós have a reputation

Tolcsva Bor
3934 Tolcsva, Táncsics utca 3
T: +36 47 384 188
M: +36 20 9384 188

for paying great attention to detail in their winemaking, in both the vineyard and cellar. We admired their 2003 6-Puttonyos Aszú and the remarkable 1993 Aszú-Eszencia.

THE FAMILY WELCOMES visitors by appointment to the winery and to their small panzió, with rooms at modest prices. This is well-worth knowing in a town with few other accommodation possibilities.

PAULECZKI-VIN

Pauleczki-Vin
3934 Tolcsva, Bajcsy-Zsilinszky utca 14
T & F: +36 47 384 026
M: +36 30 412 0512
dr.pauleczki@enternet.hu
www.pauleczki-vin.hu
Directions: As for Oremus.

ANTAL PAULECZKI SR., who devoted his life to Tokaji wine, has handed over the family business to his son and daughter. Grandson Adam is now starting his viticultural studies.

PAULECZKI WORKS 45 hectares in First Growth vineyards such as Kincsem, Mandulás, and Szentvér, planted with Furmint, Hárslevelű, Yellow Muscat and also Muscat Ottonel. They have a particular feel for Muscat (of both varieties) and produce delightfully aromatic wines by traditional methods.

THE WINERY AND VISITOR facilities have recently been modernised and reflect the family's confidence in the future of well-made Tokaji wines. The new cellar is very attractive, and we admired their 1993 Aszú-Eszencia made by traditional methods.

FITOMARK 94

BOTH DR. ISTVÁN KISS and his wife are highly qualified horticulturalists, passionate about making fine Szamorodni and Aszú wines in the

> **Fitomark 94**
> 3934 Tolcsva, Arany János utca 16a
> T: +36 47 536 400
> M: +36 30 911 9274
> kissbor@axelero.hu

traditional manner from their 15 hectares, many of them is in the First Growth Kincsem Vineyard.

THE KISS FAMILY has an esteemed reputation for their Furmint and Cuvee wines, which are available in many local restaurants and wine shops and can be purchased through the Internet. People still talk about the coveted 1972 Aszú 6-Puttonyos.

BABITS

THE BABITS FAMILY traces its origins to the 13th century, when King Béla IV encouraged Italian settlers to Tokaj with grants of land. So many Italians came that the region became known as 'Little Italy', as the nearby village named Olaszliszka ('Italian Liszka') indicates.

THE 22.5-HECTARE estate is run by László Babits Jr. Furmint and Hárslevelű are planted in Kincsem; eight hectares are devoted to Yellow Muscat in Poklos; and Kövérszőlő, which is increasingly used, is planted in Vay.

THE ASZÚ WINES, made in the traditional way, are matured for longer than usual in large oak barrels, and have a wonderful deep-golden colour and mature, round flavours.

WHEN VISITING THE WINERY, try and find time to walk up to the top of the Poklos Vineyard, because you will have spectacular views of the Bodrog flood plain – the cause of the early-morning mists so essential to the botrytisation process.

> **Babits**
> 3934 Tolcsva, Arany János utca 31
> T: +36 47 384 248
> **Directions:** The winery is at Szegi, just off Road 37 between Szegi and Szegilong, opposite the Tornyos Wine House. Tour and tasting by appointment. Food is available if ordered in advance.

SÁROSPATAK

0   500 m   1000 m

Map: © Molnár Ede András 2007

Sárospatak

WHEN YOU FIRST ARRIVE in Sárospatak you will find it hard to believe that this provincial town of 15,000 souls, standing peacefully alongside the gently-flowing Bodrog River, was once described as the 'Athens of Hungary' and likened to England's university town of Cambridge.

SÁROSPATAK FIRST BECAME FAMOUS for its great Reform College, opened in 1531, where sons of the wealthy, independent-minded Hungarian aristocracy were educated alongside candidates for the Church. The school attracted some of the foremost European educators of the day, including Comenius – the renowned Moravian humanist – who taught there between 1650-54.

ATTRACTIONS

THE COLLEGE'S PRINCIPAL ATTRACTION today is the Great Library, once housing more than 75,000 volumes. Despite the ravages of war and occupation, the oval library still retains a large number of rare volumes. To visit the Great Library arrange a time with the Tour-inform office in the Sárospatak Cultural Centre, a prominent building on Eötvös utca as you come into the town centre from Road 37. There are parking places nearby and a handily placed ATM.

THE CULTURAL CENTRE was designed by Imre Makovecz, one of Hungary's more imaginative architects of the 1970s and 1980s. It is an unusual building designed like an open book, and its original, organic style ran counter to the more rigid thinking of the Communist Party at the time of its creation. Today it hosts theatre, dance and musical performances.

BY FAR THE MOST POPULAR attraction in the town is the splendidly restored Sárospatak Castle, the largest and best-preserved Renaissance castle in Hungary. For nearly 100 years from 1616, it was the home of the Rákóczi Family, who enlarged and embellished it, making it more of a palace than a fortified castle.

FOLLOWING RÁKÓCZI'S DEFEAT in the Hungarian War of Independence (1703-1711), ownership of the castle passed to first the princely Trautsohn Family, then the Bretzenheim and Windischgraetz dynasties before being acquired by the Hungarian State after WWII. Restored in the 1990s, it merits unhurried inspection.

WE RECOMMEND THE GUIDED TOUR, because it evokes the history of Hungary and one of its more remarkable families during the 16th and 17th centuries. The Hungarian National Rákóczi Museum at nearby St. Erzsébet utca 19 (T: +36 47 311 083, rakoczi.sarospatak@muzeum.hu) provides greater detail on this remarkable Hungarian family.

ALLOW YOURSELF a break to gather fresh energy for the 12-metre descent into the cool Rákóczi Cellars, running for at least a kilometre underneath the castle. Now owned by Chateaux Pajzos and Megyer, the cellars house precious Aszú wines of the very kind that the Rákóczi Princes helped to make world-famous.

AS YOU LEAVE the castle complex you will see before you the great Castle Church devoted to Saint Elizabeth, one of the most beloved of all Hungarians, who despite her royal pedigree selflessly devoted her life to the service of the poor and needy. Inside the church is one of the largest and most splendid Gothic halls in Hungary.

THE GOTHIC SÁROSPATAKI KÉPTÁR gallery at St. Erzsébet utca 14 hosts a permanent exhibition of the works of sculptor János Andrássy Kurta, as well as temporary displays.

ACCOMMODATIONS IN SÁROSPATAK

EVINOR PANZIÓ

This newly built panzió on the banks of the Bodrog, just south of the castle walls, was built to high specifications. Owned and

Evinor Panzió
3950 Sárospatak, Arad utca
T: +36 47 311 946
M: +36 30 399 55 52
evinor@hu.inter.net

operated by the Simkó Family, who own the cellars underneath, it is an excellent place to stage a tasting of the Evinor wines, as well as stay overnight. It is bound to be popular, so book early.

HOTEL BODROG

The refurbished wellness hotel, situated in the town centre, has 50 large and comfortable rooms.

Hotel Bodrog
3950 Sárospatak, Rákóczi utca 58
T: +36 47 311 744, F: +36 47 311 527
bodrog@t-online.hu, www.hotelbodrog.hu

Vár Vendéglő
3950 Sárospatak,
35 Árpád utca
T & F: +36 47 311 370
info@varvendeglo.hu
www.varvendeglo.hu

VÁR VENDÉGLŐ

The hotel, which has the look and feel of an old Hungarian csarda, is on the south bank of the Bodrog River opposite the castle. However, it has modern bedrooms and a pleasant restaurant that specialises in fresh Bodrog fish.

There are two other very good panzios in the town centre. Both the Kert (Rákóczi utca 31) and the Liget (Arany János utca 28) are welcoming and comfortable, and both have the colossal summertime advantages of having pleasant little gardens.

Two kilometres out of town, just beyond the thermal baths, there is a very good campsite. Tengerszem (T: +36 47 312 774) also rents small bungalows with bathrooms and kitchens.

DINING IN SÁROSPATAK

VÁR VENDÉGLŐ

We recommend the Vár Vendéglő's restaurant because it seems very popular with local gourmets, specialises in serving fresh fish from the provident Bodrog, and serves its well-prepared food with a smile. There is also a good selection of

| **Vár Vendéglő** |
| Sárospatak, Árpád utca 35 |
| T: +36 47 311 370 |

wines by the glass, including Zemplén Chardonnay and Sauvignon Blanc produced locally by Chateau Pajzos.

WINERIES

CHATEAU PAJZOS

THE CHATEAU PAJZOS estate spreads happily across the sunny hillsides along Road 37 past the turnoff to Tolcsva. The old manor house boasts cellars with hundreds of barrels of gently maturing Aszú wine.

WHEN THE HUNGARIAN government decided to privatise the estate in 1992 it attracted the immediate attention of the late Jean-Michel Arcaute, a great enthusiast for Tokaji wines. It is now solely owned by Jean-Louis Laborde, who is also the proprietor of Chateau Clinet in Pomerol.

LABORDE STARTED LIFE as an agricultural engineer more accustomed to bringing in food crops than wine-grape harvests. However, after Arcaute persuaded him of the advantages in the wine business, he transferred his natural affinity for the flora of his native southwest France to the vineyards of Pomerol and Tokaj.

LIKE OTHER TOP ESTATE OWNERS, Laborde understands the importance of developing viticultural practice to ensure perfectly ripe grapes. That is why he engaged Michel Rolland, his near-neighbour in Bordeaux, as consulting oenologist.

Chateau Pajzos

3950 Sárospatak, Nagy Lajos
utca 12
T: +36 47 312 310
F: +36 47 312 320
pajzosmegyer@axelero.hu
Directions: Cellar tours and
tastings take place at the
Rákóczi Cellars at Sárospatak
Castle. The entrance to the
cellars is on the right-hand
side on the approach to the
castle gates.
Owner: Jean-Louis Laborde
Estate: 68 hectares planted at
a density of 5,500 vines per
hectare on a low cordon.
Varieties planted: Furmint
50%, Hárslevelű 40%, Yellow
Muscat 10%
Visiting hours: 10:00-16:00
Tour and tasting cost:
From Ft 2,500
Languages spoken:
English, French

THE FIRST WINEMAKER WAS THOMAS LÁSZLÓ, a Canadian-Hungarian winemaker who established his reputation making delectable sweet wines at the Henry Pelham Estate in Canada.

TODAY THE OVERALL responsibility for Chateaux Pajzos and Megyer lies with András Győrffy, a graduate of Budapest Horticultural University and Cirencester Agricultural College. The chief winemaker since 1999 is Sándor Zsurki, whose grandfather planted Chateau Pajzos and whose father was vineyard manager at Oremus.

THE TWO ESTATES are no more than eight to ten kilometres apart and yet they produce entirely different wines. The soil at Pajzos is weathered andesite and warms up quickly, yielding round, generously flavoured wines. At Pajzos, the fruit aromas and flavours are enhanced by macerating the aszú berries in a base wine made exclusively from Yellow Muscat rich in organic acids.

PAJZOS MAKES a delicious range of Aszús as well as superb late-harvest Yellow Muscat and Hárslevelű wines. Its 1993 Essencia got near-perfect marks from international juries wherever it competed. In 1998 and 2003 the winery produced a distinctive and stylish ice wine.

THE WINERY ALSO PRODUCES a Zemplén Chardonnay from old vines planted during the experimental years of the communist period. This wine confirms our long-held view that almost any variety – white or red – planted in Tokaji's volcanic soils will produce an interesting and enjoyable wine.

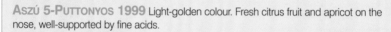

Range of Wines

LATE-HARVEST FURMINT 2003 Pale-yellow colour. Raisin aroma. Well-balanced and delicious.

LATE-HARVEST HÁRSLEVELŰ 2003 Fruity wine, its sugar well-balanced with fine acids.

LATE-HARVEST YELLOW MUSCAT 2003 Golden colour and rich, honeyed bouquet. Luscious wine.

ASZÚ 5-PUTTONYOS 1999 Light-golden colour. Fresh citrus fruit and apricot on the nose, well-supported by fine acids.

ASZÚ 6-PUTTONYOS 2000 Dried apricot bouquet. A fine and elegant wine with beautiful poise and balance.

CHATEAU PAJOS TOKAJ ESSENCIA 1993 Sensational wine. Pure nectar. Honeyed with pleasant underpinning of citrus flavours. *Wine Spectator* gave it 99/100 points.

PAJZOS VINEYARD

Pajzos is well-sited on south-facing slopes to the east of Tolcsva. The hard basalt base rock is covered with an andesite/clay soil that nourishes the Furmint, Hárslevelű, and Yellow Muscat vines and produces rich, fruity wines with concentrated flavours.
The basalt base rock and sunny disposition also ensure that the vine roots are kept warm. If the summer gets too hot, the vineyard is open to the cooling evening breezes that sweep along the Bodrog Valley floor.
The vineyard can be recognised by the old manor house that stands in its midst. The long-term plan is to renovate the house for use as a visitor centre, and to expand the barrel-ageing capacity of its cellar.

CHATEAU MEGYER

MEGYER IS A FINE estate just north of Sárospatak. It was first planted out by Count Ferenc Dobó in 1576, and later became the property of the Rákóczi Family and was classified as a First Growth vineyard.

Chateau Megyer
3950 Sárospatak,
Nagy Lajos utca 12
T: +36 47 312 310
F: +36 47 312 320
pajzosmegyer@axelero.hu
Directions:
Cellar tours and tastings take place at the Rákóczi Cellars at Sárospatak Castle. The entrance to the cellars is on the right-hand side on the approach to the castle gates.
Owner: Jean Louis Laborde (French)
Estate: 80ha under vine replanted at a density of 5,500 vines per hectare on a low cordon.
Varieties planted: Furmint, Hárslevelű, and Yellow Muscat
Tour and tasting cost: From Ft 2,500
Visiting hours: 10:00-16:00
Languages spoken: English, French

DURING THE 1990S IT WAS purchased along with Chateau Pajzos by Jean Louis Laborde. The Chateaux share winemaking facilities and the famous Rákóczi Cellars in Sárospatak that welcomes visitors daily without appointment.

DESPITE ITS PROXIMITY to Chateau Pajzos and the shared operations, Megyer has a strong personality of its own. The main differences with its sister Chateau are due to the nature of the soil and the subtle variations in the two microclimates.

THE SOIL AT MEGYER IS RHYOLITE, fine-grained volcanic rock containing crystalline fragments that foster steely wines with very firm acids. Furmint seems very happy in these soils, judging by the flavour and body of the wines which have a very big following in Central and Eastern Europe.

THE OTHER BIG DIFFERENCE is in the microclimate. Megyer is usually a degree or so cooler than Pajzos, and we believe that this is because it is closer to the Bodrog and its rhyolite soil is not as naturally warm as the black andesite and basalt in the Pajzos vineyards.

CHATEAU MEGYER ASZÚ WINES have been extremely successful in international competition. We admire their mineral-rich character and their lean and accomplished style.

Range of Wines

DRY FURMINT 2005 Fresh fruit with strong mineral tones.

MUSCAT 2004 Very successful dry vinification of this lovely grape.

LATE-HARVEST FURMINT 2005 Cool, clear, crisp Furmint with high residual sugar balanced by fine acids.

3-, 4-, AND 5-PUTTONYOS ASZÚ 2000 These superb wines are as good value-for-money as you will find anywhere.

EVINOR

SÁNDOR SIMKÓ is an experienced winemaker who was at Chateau Pajzos for several years. He takes good care of his Furmint, Hárslevelű and Muscat vines to produce vigorous wines that reflect the mineral character of the volcanic soils. He makes his Aszú wines in the classical style, and his Aszú 6-Puttonyos 2000 has recently been exported to China.

EVINOR ALSO OWNS a few hectares of Chardonnay, Sauvignon Blanc, and Pinot Gris (called Szürkebarát in Hungary) that are not entitled to the Tokaji appellation. Such varietal wines do not represent a new departure for Tokaj – the vines were planted for research purposes during the communist period, and will be replaced with authorised varieties when they come to the end of their life.

IN SUMMER 2007 the Simkós opened a brand-new, top-quality panzió above their old cellar on the banks of the Bodrog River, below the south wall of Sárospatak Castle. Tastings can be arranged in the cellars or on the veranda of the new panzió. This significant private development reveals the confidence that local producers have in the future of wine tourism. We expect this panzió to be very busy so book well in advance.

Evinor
3950 Sárospatak, Bercsényi út 27
T & F: +36 47 312 234
evinor@hu.inter.hu
www.evinor.hu
Directions: To the winery – from Tokaj take Roads 38 and 37 to Sárospatak. Turn off at the roundabout for Sárospatak. Bercsényi is the third right turn after the petrol station. To the cellars and panzió – proceed into Sárospatak, turn right at the traffic lights, and continue through another set of lights for 800 metres with the castle wall on your left. Then turn left to follow the castle wall south. The new panzió overlooks the Bodrog and the cellars are underneath.
Owner: Sándor and Mária Simkó
Estate: 19ha mainly in Kincsem, Királyhegy, and Zsadány
Varieties planted: Furmint, Hárslevelű and Yellow Muscat
Languages spoken: German

KINCSEM VINEYARD

The vineyards around the old Waldbott residence, Kincsem Kastély, are some of the most attractive in the region. The open hills have perfect exposure to the sun and are close enough to the Bodrog flood plain to benefit from the misty mornings that create the best conditions for botrytis. A good track runs off the road up to the mansion (now in disrepair) from where you can clearly see the low-lying water meadows.

In the days when Sárospatak was the political and economic centre of the region, the busy main road from Budapest divided the estate, and the parts of the vineyard became known as 'above' and 'below' the Sárai Road. Today, the entire vineyard is above Road 37.

Named after the invincible Hungarian racehorse, the vineyard is indeed a treasure yielding exceptional wines with rich fruit and firm acidity.

Many different owners have plots in Kincsem. However, for the Simkós it is a very special vineyard where the Yellow Muscat flourishes, adding wonderfully rich aromas and flavours to their wines.

OTHER WINERIES IN SÁROSPATAK, HERCEGKÚT AND SÁTORALJAÚJHELY

ESTABLISHED IN SÁROSPATAK IN 1999, the Heidrich Winery has eight hectares of fine vineyards producing very acceptable wines that are mostly sold locally.

IN NEARBY HERCEGKÚT, the cooperative there is a well-respected producer, while the privately owned Götz Winery, with 16.5 hectares to harvest, is on the old Gomboshegyi cellar row, a reminder of the days when there were many other wineries in the area. Götz makes some fine Aszú wines with generous proportions of Yellow Muscat.

SÁTORALJAÚJHELY, the largest and most important town in the region, boasts some of the oldest Tokaji cellars – dating back to the 12th century. The Ungvár Cellar Row, now a World Heritage Site, is still home to a number of family wineries, including Bodnár, Evinest and Köveshegy. Dr. Sándor Bodnár, leader of his family firm, is one of the most experienced Tokaji winemakers who takes a special pride in his late-harvest Hárslevelű.

TOKAJI AROUND THE WORLD

FOLLOWING THE TRIANON TREATY OF 1920, Hungary lost two-thirds of its territory. Transylvania became part of Romania and large parts of the Felvidék (Upper Hungary) first became part of the Czechoslovakia and then Slovakia.

PART OF THE TERRITORY that is now Slovakia includes about 178 hectares of land once entitled to the Tokaji Appellation. Most of it now belongs to the Slovenske Nove Mesto Cooperative, which still makes Tokaji wines in the traditional manner. Their methods predate those used by Hungarian winemakers working for the Borkombinát; for example there was no heavy pasteurisation of the wines, nor were they strengthened by the addition of alcohol.

HOWEVER, there is evidence that there are substantial differences between the Slovakian vineyard soils and those of Tokaji south of the border. There is more limestone and sandstone, and the microclimate is less conducive to botrytisation. It seems that vines were originally planted here in the 1890s as part of the research programme dedicated to developing disease-resistant rootstock during the phylloxera crisis.

THE HUNGARIAN AND SLOVAKIAN governments have reached sensible agreement that in the future, wines of Tokaji appellation should be made from classified areas and according to Hungarian wine law.

THERE HAVE ALSO BEEN agreements with authorities in other parts of the wine world where the Tokaj name was used to denote either grape varieties or wine styles. In Italy, Tocai Fruilano has long been produced as a dry white wine in the Fruili area of the Veneto region, but EU law has regulated that the name Tocai should be discontinued from March 2007.

TOKAJ VINES were first introduced into Alsace in the 16th century and were widely planted. From March 2007 they will be referred to as Pinot Gris.

IN AUSTRALIA, 'Tokay' has been the name traditionally used for Muscatel varieties, first introduced by a Hungarian immigrant in the 1850s. However, in 2005 a bilateral trade agreement between Australia and the EU determined that the name could only be used outside Europe up until 2015.

THERE WERE ALSO SOME ISSUES over the use of the Tokaji name in California, but these have now been resolved and the Tokaji name has now been given full protection throughout the wine world.

TOKAJI IN BUDAPEST

WE HOPE THAT YOU HAVE ENJOYED reading this Companion and will find it useful on visits to Tokaj. However, if you are visiting Hungary's capital and do not have time to travel up to Tokaj, we have some suggestions for enjoying Tokaji wines in Budapest.

WHERE BUDAPEST MAGAZINE, freely available in most hotels and tourist offices, lists Budapest's leading wine bars and restaurants, and here are a few suggestions of our own.

CAFÉ KÖR (WWW.CAFEKOR.COM) on Sas utca, close to St Stephen's Basilica, was one of the first wine bar/restaurants to offer a good selection of top-quality Hungarian wines by the glass. Its small, friendly tables spill out onto the street in summertime, and we like it for that chirpy kind of ambiance that raises the spirits after a morning spent sightseeing.

THE CSALOGÁNY RESTAURANT at Csalogány utca 26 (T: +36 1 255 4728) on the Buda side is a good choice for tasting fine Tokaji wines by the glass in a restaurant environment. Even master winemaker István Szepsy's wines are offered by the glass.

ANOTHER WINE BAR/RESTAURANT made for bibulous travellers is Klassz at Andrássy út 41 (T: +36 1 413 1545), where patrons have the choice of standing informally at the wine bar or sitting on high stools to taste a range of wines while enjoying tapas. At the last count there were 15 Tokaji wines listed.

ANDANTE BORPATIKA ('wine pharmacy') at Bem rakpart 2, close to the Széchenyi (Chain) Bridge on the Buda side, has a cosy club-like atmosphere and also offers a fine array of Tokaji wines to taste with delicious cold snacks, while taking in superb views of the Parliament building across the Danube.

THE NUMBER OF TOP-CLASS RESTAURANTS in Budapest with well-chosen wine lists has increased dramatically in recent years. The world-famous Gundel Restaurant, close to Heroes' Square, is a wonderful venue for lunch or dinner. If you are planning a longer stay in Budapest we suggest that you check the Gundel Website (www.gundel.hu) for details of their candlelit wine dinners held in their spacious wine cellars below the restaurant. At such monthly dinners, a leading vintner is invited to introduce the wines accompanying each course.

THIS HAS NOW BECOME A FORMAT favoured by other leading hotels such as the Corinthia Grand Hotel Royal, Corinthia Aquincum, and the Four Seasons Hotel Gresham Palace in its magnificent Páva ('Peacock') restaurant. We can highly recommend such wine-dinners because of their wonderful food-and-wine matching, and the very reasonable costs per person.

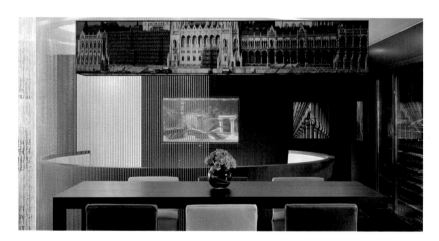

SOFITEL, THE ACCOR GROUP'S prestige hotel brand, pays special attention to Tokaji wines. Its sophisticated Paris-Budapest Café has an excellent wine list, while its sister brand Hotel Mercure on Kecskeméti utca has a dedicated Tokaji restaurant that features fine and rare Tokaji wines by the glass.

LE MÉRIDIEN HOTEL ALSO boasts the first-class Le Bourbon restaurant, where you will find a good selection of Tokaji wines in a sophisticated environment. The newly opened Peppers! restaurant in the Budapest Marriott sets out to create a relaxing atmosphere in which to enjoy its Mediterranean cuisine. Peppers! features many of the best, but lesser-known, Hungarian wines on its carefully selected wine list.

THE NUMBER OF WINE SHOPS in Budapest has also multiplied over the last few years, but the Budapest Wine Society ('Bortársaság' in Hungarian; www.bortarsasag.hu) remains one of the most dependable and has a wide selection of the very best Tokaji wines which they will ship to your home address, postal authorities permitting.

MONARCHIA ON KINIZSI UTCA (www.monarchiaborok.hu) features the wines of brilliant Tokaji winemakers such as István Szepsy and Zoltán Demeter (Királyudvar). American visitors will find Monarchia helpful for ordering fine Hungarian wines distributed in the USA by Monarchia Matt International.

FOR THOSE KEEN TO TASTE BEFORE BUYING, THE HOUSE OF HUNGARIAN WINES (T: +36 1 212 1031; www.magyarborokhaza.hu), opposite the Hilton Hotel in Budapest's Castle District, stocks a wide selection of Tokaji wines, which you can taste for a reasonable admission fee that entitles visitors to sample all kinds of Hungarian libations. Dusóczky is just one of the Tokaji wineries whose wines can be purchased there.

THREE TOKAJI PRODUCERS HAVE tasting facilities in Budapest – Aureum at Belgrád rakpart 19 (T: +36 1 483 1904), Pannon Tokay at 1-3 Daróci út (T: +36 1 381 400), and Krisztián Ungváry through his distributor Bortársaság (T: +36 1 212 2569).

HOWEVER, IF YOU HAVE BEEN ENJOYING yourself in Hungary so much that you have not left sufficient time for shopping, do not despair. The shops at Budapest Airport are well-stocked with Tokaji wines and Hungarian goose liver, the most cherished gifts to take home, and you can bring them on board the plane in sealed bags.

SELECTED BIBLIOGRAPHY

ALKONY, LÁSZLÓ: TOKAJ-THE WINE OF FREEDOM, SPREAD 2000
BOTOS, ERNŐ PÉTER & MARCINKÓ, FERENC: TOKAJ WINE ATLAS
BROADBENT, MICHAEL: VINTAGE WINE, LITTLE, BROWN 2005
COPP, DAVID: HUNGARY-ITS FINE WINES AND WINEMAKERS, 2006
HOWKINS, BEN: TOKAJI, INTERNATIONAL WINE & FOOD SOCIETY
HULOT, MATHILDE: VINS DE TOKAJ, EDITIONS FERET 2001
JOHNSON, HUGH: STORY OF WINE, MITCHELL BEAZLEY 1989
JOHNSON, HUGH & ROBINSON, JANCIS: WORLD ATLAS OF WINE
LIDDELL, ALEX: THE WINES OF HUNGARY, MITCHELL BEAZLEY 2003
ROBINSON, JANCIS: VINES, GRAPES AND WINE, MITCHELL BEAZLEY
ROBINSON, JANCIS Ed.: OXFORD COMPANION TO WINE
ROHÁLY, GÁBOR & MÉSZÁROS GABRIELLA: TERRA BENEDICTA
SZABÓ, JÓZSEF & TÖRÖK, STEPHEN: TOKAJ ALBUM, PEST 1867

ALL THE ABOVE BOOKS (EXCEPT VINS DE TOKAJ) are published in English. László Alkony, founder of *Borbarát Magazine*, has written extensively on Tokaj and his book *The Wine of Freedom* is a classic. We can also highly recommend the *Tokaj Album* reprinted in 1994 from the original 1857 text. In 2006 Péter Botos and Ferenc Marcinkó published an excellent *Atlas of Tokaj*. Ben Howkins's monograph is still current, and although Mathilde Hulot's text in *Vins de Tokaj* is in French, Patrick Cronenberger's beautiful photographs tell the story well. Alex Liddell, Gábor Rohály and David Copp have written books about all the Hungarian wine regions, devoting much of their space to Tokaj.

HUGH JOHNSON OBE, JANCIS ROBINSON OBE/MW, AND MICHAEL BROADBENT MW have all written or edited reference books that no wine writer would want to be without. We are also grateful those other personalities and authors that have helped our understanding of Tokaji.

ACKNOWLEDGEMENTS

WE ARE ETERNALLY GRATEFUL to Nick Robertson for his constructive comments and his sheer professionalism in editing this book. We also want to thank contributor Robert Smyth, and picture editor Bianca Otero, an enormous enthusiast for her work who has been well-supported by photographer Fekete K. Anna Lőrincz and Zsolt Zimmermann's design and layout work is both dynamic and stimulating. Péter Wunderlich, the tireless, leading-edge production manager, is a pleasure to work with. We sincerely thank publisher András Wiszkidenszky for leading the project from start to finish. His hard-working PA Andrea Nagy has always been helpful in getting things done.

WE ARE ALSO GRATEFUL to all those authors and winemakers who have lit up the Tokaj path before us. We have acknowledged the main authors in the bibliography but would like to thank all those other writers and vintners who we have communicated with about Tokaji. In particular we reiterate our thanks to Hugh Johnson OBE for writing the foreword. Hugh was one of the very first to invest time and money in Tokaj after the communist period and he remains as great an enthusiast for the region as ever. His help and encouragement is much appreciated.

INDEX